AF230573

A Southern Lady in Cow Country: A Love Story

Lucy Foster Miller's memoir of a life on a West Texas ranch with Clay Espy Miller

Edited by: Beth Byerley Francell

Copyright © 2025 Beth Francell, Miller Family.
Images courtesy of: Miller Family, Fort Davis Historical Society, Beth Francell, Larry Francell, Carolyn Miller, Michele Miller Browning, Jim and Sally Espy

This book or any portion thereof may not be reproduced or used in any manner whatsoever without the express written permission of the publisher or author, except for the use of brief quotations in a book review. At no time will AI or AI-related learning systems be allowed to review, scan, or scrape this book and information contained within.

Printed in the United States of America

First Printing May 2026

Paperback ISBN 978-1-959600-10-7

Hardback ISBN 978-1-959600-11-4

Purple Feather Press
Georgetown, TX 78628
www.PurpleFeatherPress.com

Table of Contents:

INTRODUCTION

by Beth Byerley Francell

Lucy Conoly Foster Miller was my maternal grandmother. I have had her manuscript since the 1980s when she wrote it. I was hesitant to publish it for anyone outside the family. I found it fascinating and revealing about our family dynamics. Despite many hardships and obstacles, Espy and Lucy were devoted to family and created a legacy. I enjoyed many happy times at their home in Fort Davis and at the ranch. Our grandparents made it happy for their nine grandchildren. They were so proud of us and cherished our unique personalities. They taught us how to "make do," a good lesson to learn.

My grandmother fit the profile of a proper Southern Lady. She considered public displays of emotion improper, though she could bring tears, and hugs and kisses with abandon. She was kind and gracious to everyone, no matter their social status. Family honor, reputation and history were prized. Family needs came first above her own interests. Her primary responsibility was her home and children. Supporting her husband in all his endeavors and presenting a united front in public fulfilled a life goal of many women at that time which was to be married.

Her great skills were cooking, gardening, decorating and entertaining. After showing her children her steadfast love, teaching them morals, manners, and discipline was job one. Propriety involved maintaining a polished public appearance. Her dress and behavior reflected modesty and refinement. Church attendance and involvement were central to her identity and social standing. She was the perfect hostess for community gatherings, weddings and funerals and always introduced newcomers to the community.

She was the inheritor of 75 years of women's involvement in causes such as abolition, temperance, and women's vote and rights. She was educated, well-read and a great conversationalist. Her hard work shaped the family home, the household, the community and her cultural identity. A lifelong Democrat, she felt that Democracy was the highest form of government.

Raised in deeply Southern Marlin, Texas, in a large extended family with mostly male cousins, Lucy was an only child. Her family began calling her Daughter, then so did her husband, children, her grandchildren and great grandchildren. Another Southern tradition was racism. We all learn from the environment we grow up in. Stereotyping nationalities and "races" were common. Daughter believed in Anglo-Saxon superiority and thought Black people needed help and discipline to thrive.

Marlin was a slave economy, cotton farming community in the fertile Brazos River bottoms. Servants replaced slaves and Jim Crow laws prevailed. In 1967, the summer after my freshman year at Trinity University, I took an opportunity to prove her wrong. Trinity sponsored Crossroads Africa, and I was assigned to go to Ghana in West Africa to build a school with 15 North American and 15 Ghanaian college students. That summer, I learned there was only one race, the human race. My contemporary Africans were exceptionally intelligent and quite well informed about world affairs and contemporary US politics.

Throughout my young-adult years of college and first jobs, Daughter wrote me long letters at least monthly with advice and news related to our interests. She wrote frequent letters to all her family members and many close friends. She was a skilled writer and often joked about someday writing the "Great American Novel." When we came to visit from Midland for holiday gatherings, she would greet us with enthusiasm and leave us with a lipstick kiss on our cheek. She read to us regularly from classic children's literature. The house smelled of fresh flowers and delicious things to eat. I loved helping her cook and garden. By the time I married, I was skilled at making cookies, candy and cakes but not much else.

She instilled my love of growing plants. She was known for taking flowers to sick people and shut-ins and providing two large arrangements for the Church each Sunday. She rose early and went to the garden to cut fresh flowers which she conditioned by removing lower leaves and soaking them in buckets of cold water. Fort Davis mornings were always cool and the best time to work. Daughter passed along the art of beautifully arranging flowers to her daughter Lucy.

She propagated geranium cuttings and seedlings in four large cold frames Espy constructed. They faced south and were angled 45 degrees, our parallel on the planet, so they received maximum solar gain and never required supplemental heat. Many flowers she kept going for years with reseeding annuals (Nasturtium, Larkspur, Stock, Bells of Ireland, Zinnias) and hardy perennials (Peonies, Baby's Breath, Iris and Daisies.) Many visits from family and friends gave her "pass along plants." Her mint patch was fertilized with "Cheer" detergent phosphate enriched gray wash water.

Gardening for her was all about sharing the beauty and the bounty. Her lilacs and peonies are still found all over town. She composted leaves, clippings and manure in Alamo creek, fertilized with manure, fed food waste to feral cats, kept a garden journal of what she planted, and was dedicated to saving water by flooding her "waffle" beds only as needed to keep them alive until it rained. She helped maintain a large garden of fruit and vegetables at the ranch where there was a canning machine to "put up the crop." She had perfect aim with a hand-made hoe to remove weeds. That hoe became the cane she needed later in life. I remember the great flower fragrances and the feeling of being helpful to her as her joints became more crippled with arthritis. I learned from her that depression could be relieved by hard work in the garden and being in nature. I learned to enjoy time reading as a great reward and restful relaxation to renew energy.

After I was born, my mother was ill, possibly postpartum depression. She (Mary Elizabeth "Betty" Miller Byerley) brought me back from San Diego to Fort Davis to have help during her recovery. I was their first grandchild and much doted on. I learned how to walk between my maternal and paternal grandmothers. Though Ruth Byerley died when I was three, I have a strong memory of being surrounded by love in this old house where we have now lived since 1997. I always felt a closeness to Daughter in our mutual interests in history, genealogy, politics, antiques, reading and gardening. She read widely in literature, history, and contemporary journalism. Many lively discussions took place in her parlor and on her Campmeeting porch between ranchers, astronomers, birders, geologists and friends, all refreshed on cake and iced tea.

Staying at the ranch for summer visits after I finished my session at Mitre Peak Girl Scout Camp was great fun. My grandfather, Espy, wanted us all to learn to ride. He had us moving cattle with him when we were very young. He had an old white mule that would tolerate seven children climbing and falling all over him. We would hitch him to a little two wheeled sulky cart to ride around ranch roads. As long as we watched out for snakes, were protected from sunburn with hats and long sleeves, and did not run down mountainsides, we had total freedom.

We swam in an old stock tank fed by a bountiful spring and were taught never to waste water. Having Depression era parents and grandparents was a good background for acquiring a conservation ethic. We also acquired a love of this desert land and its flora and fauna. My grandfather and his brother Keesey Miller began acquiring the Miller ranch in 1935. Now there are over 70 heirs. Drought has put a temporary halt to cattle raising and even decreased game hunting. Aoudad hunting provides some income. Our cousins all have a deep appreciation for this land and our family ranch legacy that marked its 100 years anniversary in November 2025.

The following is a great love story and a vivid picture of days gone by.

Many thanks to my Aunt Lucy and her son Dave and my mother for preserving, transcribing and typing Daughter's manuscript. Uncle Clay provided his memories and insights. My husband, Larry, helped with photos and historical footnotes little knowing that in reviving the Museum of the Big Bend he was following in Espy's footsteps preserving the history of this great region. Daughter-in-law Marni did a final close proof reading. Our niece Heather created this beautiful publishable document. Her skills, talents, and knowledge were invaluable. We all thank dear Daughter for the opportunity to learn from her life story.

- January 22, 2026

Clay Espy Miller October 23, 1895 - March 12, 1960

A Southern Lady in Cow Country: A Love Story

Clay Espy Miller was born October 23, 1895 at McAnnelly's Bend of the Colorado River in San Saba County, Texas. His parents, Walter Spurgeon Miller and Lena Elizabeth Espy had been married there on December 30, 1891. He was the second child. A daughter, Rosalie, had been born October 7, 1892 and had died October 1893.

Both Walter Miller and Lena Espy were descended from generations of pioneers. The Espys were French Huguenots who were driven out of France after the Revocation of the Edict of Nantes. They took refuge first in Scotland, and when the persecution of Protestants became intolerable there, fled to County Antrim, Ireland. From there they emigrated to America sometime early in the 18th Century.

The Espy Family in America [1] records the purchase of land by Josiah Espy (1699-1760) in Lancaster County, Pennsylvania in 1745. With the sole exception, Espy was descended from the father of this Josiah in a straight line of eight generations. The Espy genealogy also notes that these ancestors handed down to their descendants "the firm conviction that the Presbyterian form was the only way in which a Christian could worship".

Espy's great-grandfather, Dr. Thomas Huling Espy, came to Texas about 1838, married in 1842, went to California with the 49ers,

---

1 Espy, Florence Mercy. History and Genealogy of the Espy Family in America. No publisher listed, 1905. (Reprint: Legare Street Press).

returned to Texas and settled in Burnet County, where he lived until his death in 1896.

Burnet County was the scene of heavy Indian fighting in the years following the Civil War, and the Espy cabin was in the thick of the fray. Thomas Huling Espy, although a well-educated doctor, became a government mail contractor in his early years in Burnet County and later engaged in farming and ranching. His sixth child Henry Clay Espy (born Feb. 11, 1849) married Rowena Marley (born 1848) in 1872. Their second child, Lena Elizabeth Espy was born March 20, 1874.

The Marleys were another pioneer family whose history follows one of the familiar trails of the pioneers, from Delaware to North Carolina to Tennessee to Texas. Robert Marley (born 1815) and his wife, Virginia Hughes (born 1819) were married in Smith County, Tennessee in 1836 and emigrated to Texas with six children in 1855. He bought land from Robert D. McAnnelly at "The Bend" in the Colorado River. Two more children were born in Texas. The sixth child of this couple, Rowena Amelia Marley, became the wife of Henry Clay Espy.

The Millers were a North Carolina family who came to North Texas before the Civil War and founded the town of Denison. The log cabin of John Kimsey Miller (born 1826) and Arrena Tabor Miller (born 1829) is now preserved as a museum in Denison. This couple had 14 children, the second of whom was John Rickman Miller (born 1850).

During the Civil War, a family named Mallory fled from Missouri to Texas. Their home had been destroyed by the Yankees, and the father and two brothers had been killed in the Confederate Army. In Denison the mother, a daughter, Lucy Mandy (born 1849) and a son, Ben, were taken in and cared for by the Miller family. Shortly after their arrival in Texas, the mother died, but the children continued to live with the Miller family. On May 26, 1869 John Rickman Miller and Lucy Mandy Mallory were married. They had three sons, Walter Spurgeon Miller (born Jan. 6, 1871); Otis Leon Miller (born Apr. 30, 1873) and John Kimsey Miller (born June 2, 1875).

John Rickman Miller was a fire-eating Baptist preacher and a mighty debater of religion. He was also a high tempered family tyrant, as were many men of his generation. His wife was a sweet, gentle woman, of whom her grandson, Espy, often said, "She was the best person I ever knew."

In that era, preachers were rarely paid, so had to have other means of making a living. John Rickman was an expert carpenter and cabinet maker. It is doubtless from him that the family talent for mechanics and skill with tools was inherited. He must also have been an enterprising business man, for he managed to amass and to lose a considerable fortune during his lifetime.

He moved his family to San Saba in the 1880's and in 1900 moved to what is now Lynn County, Texas, and acquired large tracts of land around Tahoka and the present City of Lubbock. He founded the First Baptist Church of Lubbock. He was a well-educated man and was able to give his sons an education. [2]

Walter Miller was an early graduate of Baylor University – a classmate of Gov. Pat Neff. After his marriage to Lena Espy, Walter Miller taught mathematics at Howard Payne College in Brownwood, Texas.

The year 1890 marks the closing of the frontier, but these hardy pioneers did not know that, for in 1891 Henry Clay Espy was still moving West, in search of land for his cattle and health for himself. He came to the Davis Mountains in 1891 with his wife, Rowena, and their five unmarried children, Jim, Joe, Kate, Sargie, and Robert Henry (always called "Judge") and with 27 horses and 47 head of cattle. The family ranched in Willow Canyon, but later moved to Ft. Davis.

They are said to be the first family to live "on the line" [3] after the departure of the soldiers. Henry Clay Espy had already developed tuberculosis, and during a trip, on horseback, back to San Saba in the fall of 1892, made at least partly for the purpose of urging his daughter, Lena, and her husband to move to Ft. Davis, he contracted pneumonia from the exposure, and died in January, 1893 in No. 14. "on the line."

It was three years later, 1898, however, after the death of their first child and birth of their second, that Walter and Lena Miller and their six month old son, Espy, made the move to Ft. Davis. Three families, the McAnnelly's, the Buchanams, and the Millers, each with one young child made the trek together.

Dee McAnnelley kept a diary of their five-week journey, which still exists. The Millers reached Ft. Davis April 11, 1896, with all their

2 John Rickman Miller became the first salaried preacher of the existing church – Clay Espy Miller, Jr.; I don't believe he was an ordained minister – Lucy Miller Jacobson.

3 "On the line," refers to the thirteen homes for officers on the west side of the Parade Ground at Fort Davis. The property on which the Fort was located was owned privately and when the post was abandoned in July 1891 it reverted to the original owners who then rented the homes to families.

*"The Line" or Officer's Row, Image courtesy of
Fort Davis National Historic Site*

earthly possessions loaded in a covered wagon, drawn by two horses. Mr. Miller once told me that he had five dollars in his pocket when they reached Ft. Davis, and that he spent $3.85 of it to buy "the Madam" a pair of shoes. This was typical of the unselfishness that characterized his entire life.

He was not, as most of the Espys and Marlyes had been, a cattleman, but a quiet studious man of keen mind and good education and with the refinement and sensitivity of his gentle mother, Lucy Mandy Mallory. He was better suited for school teaching than for cowpunching in this rough, harsh mountain country. But his wife was unhappy away from her people, so he moved to the frontier town where the Espy family was living, and resolutely set about making a living for his wife and child.

He took whatever jobs offered, at first hauling salt and freight, later working as a cowpuncher on the L.C. Brite and W.T. Jones ranches. Two stories from this period of his life tell much about his character. His son, Keesey, recalls how Charlie Jones (brother-in-law of W.T. Jones) complained to him in later years that "he nearly worked himself to death, when he and Walter worked for Bill Jones just trying to keep up with

Walter!" Many years later, Mrs. L.C. Brite said to Espy, on being told that his youngest grandson was named Walter, "Walter Miller! He was the most honest man who ever worked for us!"

When Walter Miller worked for Bill Jones, his family lived at the Kelly Ranch, a far more isolated spot then, than it has become since the advent of good roads. A cowpuncher's working day was from before sun-up till after dark, so Mrs. Miller and little Espy were alone in the house for many hours every day. She was terribly afraid, especially of Mexicans, who looked like the Indians her forebears had fought in Burnet County.

One day a Mexican wandered by and demanded food of her. She handed out food to him, then watched from the house till he was gone. When he was out of sight, she took her child and fled to the top of the woodpile, where, armed with the axe, she could watch in all directions. There her husband found them when he returned home after dark.

Meanwhile, her mother, "Mammy" Espy, and two unmarried sons, Jim and Judge, had "squatted" on free land at Lobo. Adobe shacks were built on adjoining corners of section lines. A four-year term of residence in one of these guaranteed ownership of the land. [4]

The Espy daughters had both married in 1896, Kate to Zee Finley and Sargie to Lee Prude. Joe Espy had married Lola Pruitt in 1900 and had gone to live on the Horse Thief Ranch, north of Ft. Davis, which he had bought with a $12,000 inheritance from her father's estate.

Somewhere about this time, Walter Miller had gone to work for Whittaker Keesey in the store the latter had built in Valentine. This job was better suited to his abilities than cowpunching, and he managed the store successfully. His younger brother, J.K. Miller (called "Bub") and his wife, "Tine" moved to Valentine to work for him in the store, and his parents also lived there briefly.

On January 15, 1902, the second son of Walter and Lena Miller was born in Valentine and was named John Keesey Miller. Espy started to school in Valentine when he was five years old. His most vivid memory of his first school days was his anguish when the big boys stole his cap.

4 "Lobo" refers to the area a few miles north of Valentine towards VanHorn; "My father always referred to them as "tie houses" with walls built of discarded railroad ties.", Clay Espy Miller, Jr.

Walter S. and Lena Espy Miller with son Espy

The years in Valentine were relatively easy ones. Valentine was a section division on the Southern Pacific Railroad, and a thriving community, dominated by two mercantile establishments – the Keesey General Store and the Bell Saloon. Walter's job was a good one and the family enjoyed greater comfort and security than before.

Though the Millers were Baptists, a regular visitor in the home was the Rev. W.B. Bloys, on his missionary circuit to Valentine. They had other friends, among them the Conrings the Burtons and the Perrys.

The latter were an English couple, who lived for many years on their isolated ranch (now the Dick Henderson Ranch) on the Rim Rock [5] southwest of Valentine. Mr. Perry was a "remittance man" – a younger son of a titled family. Money, books and various luxuries came to their ranch home which the Perrys maintained as a little bit of England.

During Espy's childhood, the Millers often went to the Perry Ranch for overnight visits. Later the title descended to Mr. Perry, and he returned to England to claim it, but was so unhappy there that eventually he came back to the ranch to live out the rest of his life and to be buried high on a mountain behind his home.

The Millers also visited the Holland Ranch and ZH Canyon, and Kodak pictures exist of a picnic in ZH Canyon in company with the Conrings. The ranch was then owned by John Holland of Alpine, though its original owner had been Jim Hyler, [6] whose rude cabin used to stand on the south side of the box canyon behind ZH Canyon. His brand ZH gave the name to the large canyon behind which borders Vieja Pass.

John Holland owned only a few sections around the spring in ZH Canyon, but Espy said that his cattle were accustomed to grazing for a hundred miles in the unfenced flats south of the railroad. He built the ranch house, we think, and lived there part of the time and part in Alpine. He was a notorious drunkard and gunman, who killed an undetermined number of men.

One of his victims was a man named Hanley, whom he murdered, in what is now our horse pasture, in a quarrel over water rights. Espy remembered his father going out in the delivery wagon from the store and bringing back Hanley's body. He did not remember John Holland, but he always remembered the ranch house, with a row of black locust saplings growing on a ditch of water, fed by the Spring in ZH Canyon, encircling it. From that time on, it was his ambition to own that ranch, that ditch of water and those trees.

5 "The Rim Rock" refers to the west portion of the Sierra Vieja mountains which is a series of cliffs dropping down into the Rio Grande Valley. The path through the mountains from the Rio Grande Valley is Sierra Vieja Pass, where the ranch headquarters and Camp Holland are located.
6 Hyler ran cattle on the land but never took title to any of it – Clay Espy Miller, Jr.

There was also visiting back and forth with "Mammy's" family at Lobo and with the Lee Prudes who were then ranching "under the Rim". Espy learned to ride a horse and to "make a hand" with his uncles Jim and Judge, on the Lobo ranch very early in life.

On their long rides looking after their cattle, they carried an unvarying lunch prepared by "Mammy" – cold biscuit and molasses! "Mammy" was no cook.

In those years Espy began to make the long hard horseback ride across and under the Rim to the Lee Prude ranch. He was less than ten years old, undersized and timid, and his reminiscences of these rides in the early years of our marriage used to make me cry.

It was a harsh, cruel country, and life was hard for the first settlers. Only the Strong could survive. Children were expected to carry responsibilities and endure hardships that seem almost intolerable today. They did this as a matter of course, as generations of their pioneering ancestors had done before them and did not realize the hardness of their lives.

Walter and Lena Miller were devoted, conscientious and hard-working parents, but they could not shield the oldest son from the hard realities of life in the Far West in the early years of this century. So Espy learned early to carry his full share of the work of the family, and to take pride in doing so.

Walter Miller was prospering in the Keesey store, and the family was happy in Valentine, but the old dream of the pioneers, of owning land, still held him. In 1905, in response to this dominating urge, he bought a ranch North of Sierra Blanca and moved his family there. This was farther West and far more arid country than Ft. Davis or Lobo.

The family lived in a rude shack, far from neighbors. Water for cattle and humans had to be pumped from an old "dug" well by horsepower. Walter nearly lost his life in an accident while deepening this well.

Keesey recalls how, as a child of three, he did his share of work. Seated at a safe distance, his job was to "chunk" rocks at the horse and keep him moving – and thus pumping water. Even with constant pumping the water was scarcely adequate to supply their own cattle, yet it was also hauled off by barrelfulls by neighbors who had none. This move was a disastrous venture. The desert land, drought, lack of water and of fences made ranching there bitterly hard and unrewarding.

Early Espy family in Fort Davis. Front row, left to right: Charles Prude, Gunter Prude, Keesey Miller, Rowena Marley "Mammy" Espy, Joe Finley. Back row: Sargie Espy Miller, Clay Espy Miller, Lena Espy Miller, R.H. "Judge" Espy, Kate Espy Finley, Jim Espy, Don Finley.

The problem of educating their children also worried the Millers, as it does all ranch families. Some of the wealthier families of that era solved it by employing a governess who lived with the family, but more often children were sent to stay with relations in towns. Espy was sent to Roswell, N.M. for the school term, to live with his Aunt Kate and her husband Zee Finley. Though he was only ten years old, he made the train trip alone, and it involved several changes and an overnight stay in a strange hotel – a terrifying ordeal for a timid little country boy.

Physically, he was still small for his age and so burned by constant exposure to the blazing West Texas sun and biting wind that he was nicknamed "Blackenough". In later years, he loved to tell how strangers would address him in Spanish, mistaking him for a "muchacho".

Actually, his skin, under the heavy layers of tan, was fair, and his eyes an intense blue. They were memorable eyes, piercingly direct of gaze and overshadowed by extremely thick black brows. When he was young, he had a heavy shock of black hair, but, after his service in the Navy, he began to lose this, and his naturally high forehead became more prominent. The Espy forehead I always called it, for most of the descendants had it.

It was only later that I discovered that this characteristic feature, along with the dark coloring, the tall frame and the familiar "black look" were all inherited from the Marleys, who were said to have had Indian blood. The true Espy type were sandy, reddish complexioned men of slight stature like Judge.

Espy's remaining hair turned white before middle age, but his eyebrows remained inky black all his life. The contrast was startling and unforgettable. When he was a child, his prominent forehead was out of proportion to the rest of his face, but after he attained his full stature of five feet eleven and his face became fuller with the increase in his weight, it gave an unusual distinction to his countenance. He had a beautifully straight nose, and full heavy lips. His skin, though weather beaten from life long exposure, was always perfectly clear and as smooth as a woman's. When I first knew Espy, I thought him ugly, but both his appearance and my opinion change with the years, and, as he grew older, he became a very handsome and distinguished looking man.

But to go back to his education. He spent two winters in schools in Roswell, and in the summers, went back to help out on the ranch. Walter Miller became increasingly discouraged with his ranch venture. Espy always said that his father simply did not have the temperament for ranching. He could, and did, do the hard and unceasing labor it required, but he had nothing of the gambler in his make-up, and ranching in the arid West is always a gamble. The terrible uncertainties and constant hazards of debt, drought, and depression, which are inherent in the cattle business, were more than his orderly mind could stand. So, in December 1907 he sold the ranch to Joe Gardner and moved his family back to Ft. Davis.

Prior to this, Whittaker Keesey, who had established and made a small fortune from the Union Trading Company in Ft. Davis, [7] sold the business to a group of local men. He had already sold the store in Valentine to Conring and Bunton. One of the Ft. Davis stockholders, a

7 The Union Trading Company was created in 1908 and capitalized at $40,000. The initial purchase was the Whittaker Keesey store. W.S. Miller was a partner. Eventually the Union Trading company encompassed the mercantile, the bank, and the Limpia Hotel.

Mr. Little, moved away soon after this and Walter bought his share of stock in the company. It was as a part owner of "The Union", and actual manager (though Judge J.P. Weatherby, the bookkeeper, held that title in his lifetime) that Walter Miller made his second entry into Ft. Davis, and he continued in this capacity until his death.

After the return of the family to Fort Davis, Espy began working for his uncle Joe Espy on weekends and during the summers. He used to say that he worked for his Uncle Joe 18 years, but that was stretching the truth somewhat as he spent four of those years away at school and one in the Navy. However, it is true that his youth and young manhood were very largely spent in the service of his Uncle Joe.

Joe Espy was a financial genius of a sort, a gambler by nature and possessed of the successful gambler's instinct for the "sure thing". His lucky inheritance of $12,000, from his wife's share of her father's estate, upon his marriage in 1900, gave him the necessary capital with which to lay the foundations of his fortune. He was extremely shrewd and unscrupulous in money matters, and tremendously clever at exploiting those who worked for him, his various hired men, his nephew Espy and even his own sons.

Josiah Winchester (Uncle Joe) Espy. Image courtesy of Jim and Sally Espy

Working under such a taskmaster was a hard school, but in that school, while still young and impressionable, Espy became proficient in the many and arduous skills required of a cowpuncher. As a good cowhand must be, he became jack of all trades and able to do any job on the ranch – fencing, windmill repair, feeding, herding, and doctoring cattle, shoeing horses, cutting wood, superintending long cattle drives, etc. etc.

He was still a small boy when he began to go to the Espy ranch each summer with the family to help with the chores and odd jobs, milking, chopping wood, making a garden, in addition to helping the men with cattle work. Mrs. Espy was a kind and motherly woman and was invariably good to him, and he also helped with her large family of young children.

Espy started to school in Ft. Davis under Miss Mabel Bloys (as did his two older children!), and later had a succession of men teachers. But Walter Miller was dissatisfied with the education provided by the village school, so when a persuasive Baptist preacher came along, seeking pupils for a newly founded school in Cisco, called Britton's Training School, he decided to send Espy there. Espy spent a year there, not very profitably or happily.

In 1913 he went to Simmons College in Abilene, and spent the next three years there, leaving without a degree. These were probably the happiest years of his life. Although he was not greatly benefited scholastically, for he was not studious and had an inadequate preparation for college, his vision was broadened by experiences there and especially by the friendships he formed during those carefree years. He began then to develop his capacity for friendship, which became one of his outstanding traits of character.

The friends he made at Simmons endured for life. Especially was this true of his Daman and Pythias relationship with one roommate, Tom Carson of Barstow. This must have been a case of attraction of opposites, for Espy and Tom were about as different as two men could be.

Tom was a quiet, methodical, studious boy, whose diligent scholarship took him to a Ph.D. in Physics, and later to head of the Bureau of Standards in Washington. Espy was a restless, high-spirited creature, far more eager for gay companions and wild schoolboy scrapes than for education. Perhaps each admired in the other the traits of character that he himself lacked, but the friendship was close and genuine and deepened as the years went on, in spite of the wide divergence in their lives.

Espy took an active interest in athletics, made the basketball squad and was a long-distance runner of some repute.[8] In those years he was still literally as "thin as a rail", with a thick thatch of black hair and the heavy eyebrows which were so distinctive all his life. He was quite a ladies' man and courted many girls on the campus. He had the normal

---

8 "Actually he was a sprinter having won prizes in the 100 yard and 220 yard dashes." Clay Espy Miller, Jr.

young man's keen interest in the opposite sex, but it was not until he got away from his mother's disapproving surveillance that he could pursue that interest. This is probably the main reason why the years at Simmons were such happy ones.

He was always enormously proud of the fact that in his final year at Simmons he had been elected to an exclusive secret society. The framed picture of this group for years ornamented our bedroom wall. All his life he was to look back on those years at Simmons as a brief interlude in Paradise.

Clay Espy Miller as a young man

In his last year at Simmons, his little sister, Audrey Miller was born. Espy had not gone back to Ft. Davis for the previous Christmas vacation and knew nothing of the expected arrival until he received a telegram saying, "Little Sister arrived today, and asks for a name." He promptly named her Audrey, for the girl he was currently in love with.

Whether because of lack of money or lack of interest, he left Simmons without a degree, and went to work full time for his Uncle Joe Espy. By this time, Mr. Joe had greatly expanded his ranching interests with the purchase of the Powell and Ryan ranches. Espy worked for the usual cowpuncher wages - $40 a month and board. "Board" was frijol beans and cornbread and moldy bacon, and occasionally fried meat – a diet that ruined his digestion at an early age.

During those years he "batched" at the various ranches for the Espy family had long since moved to Ft. Davis. Sometimes he had a "pardner", George or Andy Williams or one of Mr. Joe's hands or a Mexican laborer working with him. More often he was alone. At one period during this time, he was in camp for over a month with a bunch of Mexicans who were building fence. This was when his Spanish became a second language; as he told me later, "he learned to think in Mexican!"

His working hours were from dawn to dark, six days a week, and frequently seven. He was expected to cope with whatever emergencies arose on the ranch – lack of food or water, disease, drought, blizzards, windmill and fence repair, driving cattle to distant markets, and always with a minimum of help and funds.

During those years, he virtually lived in the saddle. In actual fact, Espy acted as foreman on his uncle's ranches during these years, as Mr. Joe's widening speculations in cattle took him more and more frequently away from Ft. Davis, but he was never given the dignity of a foreman's title – nor his wages!

It was a hard life and a lonely one – especially for Espy who was by nature a social animal. I think his hatred of being alone in later years stemmed from those lonely years on the Espy ranches. There were some breaks in the monotony of the constant and unremitting work – trips to Ft. Davis, Camp Meeting [9] time, and "works" on neighboring ranches. If the "work" happened to be at Mr. Beau McCutcheon's 7 Ranch, that was regarded as a lark – for there was always good food and good times there.

One small concession Mr. Joe made to his nephew during this time (actuated, no doubt, by his shrewd guess that it was the surest way to keep Espy working for him) was to allow him to pasture a few cattle on his own, on the Espy ranches. Espy had begun buying calves with the first money he earned as a small boy, and he continued to invest every cent he could save into cattle. By dent of stringent economy and the normal increase of cows, he had gradually built up a small herd of his own over the years.

When he went to war in 1918, he was obliged to sell this herd to his Uncle Joe at the prevailing low prices, as Mr. Joe's generosity and patriotism did not extend to pasturing his nephew's cattle free, while Espy was away serving his country.

9 "Camp Meeting" refers to the Bloys Campmeeting, started in 1890 as a multi-denominational (Presbyterian, Methodist, Disciples of Christ, and Baptist) assembly that meets for a week each August. Founded by the Reverend William Bloys, a circuit rider Presbyterian preacher sent to the mountains for health reasons. The Bloys Campmeeting Association operates from Skillman Grove, fifteen miles west of Fort Davis on Highway 166.

Why a dry land cowpuncher, who had rarely seen a body of water much larger than the Pecos River, should have chosen to serve in the U.S. Navy, I have never understood.

On June 12, 1918, Espy and his close friend, Kenneth Smith, enlisted in the Navy in El Paso, and were sent to bootcamp in San Diego. His year in the Navy was another enlightening experience, though hardly a happy one. He had always had a weak stomach, and he suffered agonies from sea sickness during the entire duration of his service. He came down with mumps soon after he entered bootcamp and all but died from it – in a tent on muddy ground at San Diego. His ship was the old battleship "Oregon", then on duty patrolling the Pacific Coast.

Espy, like many desert raised boys, did not know how to swim. His account of his near drowning when the raw recruits were pitched off the decks of the ship into the ocean – to sink or swim – was hair raising.

These were war times, and the Navy did not hold with coddling its recruits. Much of his term of service was spent off Coronado Island or in San Francisco harbor. He was always to remember San Francisco was the coldest spot he ever saw.

The one pleasant memory of the whole time was a joyous reunion with his old friend, Tom Carson. Tom had a commission as Ensign and was then stationed in San Francisco. He and Espy kept in touch in their years since college. One evening, when Espy got leave from his ship, he went up to Tom's apartment, when Tom dressed him up in his extra uniform (there was not such a great difference in their size then as in later years), and the two young "officers" went out on the town for a gay evening.

After his discharge from the Navy the following year, Espy returned to Fort Davis, and to his old job with his Uncle Joe. In later years, he used to say that this was the biggest mistake he ever made in his life.

And so it was, for had he started out for himself then, he would have been better off financially and in every other way. But he had sold his small herd at the prevailing low prices when he entered the Navy.

Now cattle had gone sky high, and he had not money enough to buy back a starting herd. Neither did he have the nerve to undertake the big gamble starting out on his own involved.

For Mr. Joe's most wicked trait was his deliberate effort to destroy the self-confidence of the men who worked for him. He made them feel that they were only peons, whose sole duty was to carry out his orders for incessant hard work. His principal method of doing this was to make them feel that they were not capable of making the decisions necessary to succeed in the cattle business. He did this to his own sons, as well as to his nephews and many other young men who worked for him over the years.

Espy and his other cowhands gave the best years of their lives to helping make Joe Espy's fortune, but the only benefit they got was lots of experience. Espy was restless and dissatisfied, for he knew his uncle well enough to realize that there was no future – except grueling drudgery – in working for him, but he lacked the courage to make the break and start out on his own.

Jobs were scarce following the war, and cowpunching was the only trade he knew. He used to say that he didn't think he was really cut out to be a cowpuncher, but he never had the opportunity to learn any other trade. So, he went back to work for Mr. Joe and took up his life of "batching" again.

During these years his responsibilities increased, as Mr. Joe's business enterprises widened. One of Espy's jobs was to take train loads of cattle to market in Fort Worth, Kansas City, and other cities.

This was cold, dirty, rough work, which involved going into the filthy, crowded cars whenever the train stopped to see that none of the cattle were down on the floor of the car and in danger of being trampled to death. The unfortunate ones who were down had to be "tailed up" or prodded or lifted back on their feet – a hard and dangerous task.

The cattle had to be unloaded at stated intervals along the way for food and water, then reloaded and finally had to be delivered in good condition to the buyer. Espy learned during these trips to walk on top of a moving train, watching for cattle in distress in the cars below. In his brief periods of leisure, he shared the hot little caboose with the members of the train crew.

One winter Mr. Joe leased pasturage for a herd of steers in Northern Oklahoma, near Fairfax, and sent Espy to look after the cattle for the term of the lease. The winter was a cold one, with heavy snow, but Espy's tasks were lighter than at home, for he lived in a comfortable house with the couple to whom the pasture belonged and found them friendly and congenial. The wife was a fine cook, and her good meals were a welcome change from his usual diet of bacon and beans. The husband helped him feed and care for the cattle, and their hours of leisure were spent playing bridge or visiting. It was a happy interval for the lonely young man. The ranch was in the midst of an Indian Reservation. Espy often recalled in later years how dirty the old squaws were, but how beautiful the young half-breed Indian girls were.

✛

Though Espy was a superb horseman; he was never a "Rodeo hand". He was an expert with a rope and master of all the skills required to a cowhand. But he never had the time nor the opportunity to polish those skills to the degree of perfection required of rodeo performers even in his young days, when rodeos were still largely amateur affairs.

Mr. Joe would never have permitted his hands to practice roping on his cattle, except in line of duty, and neither would Espy when he acquired cattle of his own. He not only had too much respect for their value, but he also had too much sympathy for their suffering to treat cattle as roughly as was necessary to develop the expertness a rodeo hand needed. But he loved rodeos, and though he was seldom a contestant, he was often a judge or time keeper at the early rodeos which were held on holidays all over the area.

He also loved horse racing. He did not often see professional racing, but matched races between favorite horses was one of the main diversions of early day cowhands, and Espy rode in some of these events. He was highly competitive by nature, and he had inherited his full share of the Espy's gambling instinct. He would bet on the change of the moon, and he wanted to win every game he ever played – even if it was only tiddley-winks! He loved to bet small sums on races and rodeo events, and always said that only poverty kept him from being a gambler. But it was really the prudence and steadiness of his Miller forebears that restrained him, plus the training in rigid economy he had to practice all his life.

His enjoyment of rodeos lasted most of his life, and when we began to have a little money to spend on diversions, they were his favorite entertainment. He always insisted on my accompanying him to rodeos, in which I had, after witnessing my first one, a total lack of interest. But I went with him for years, because it hurt his feelings when I did not share his pleasure in anything he liked, and because he would rather have had me go unwillingly than not to go at all. He confidently expected that I would acquire a taste for rodeos by constant exposure to them, but I never did. Nor did any of our children have any interest in the rough sport after their early childhood.

Espy liked games of every kind and had a passion for puzzles. Before our marriage when bridge became a popular pastime in Ft. Davis, he became an expert bridge player and thoroughly enjoyed the game. I had no interest in any kind of game and had never learned to play bridge.

In spite of the pressures of the dedicated bridge players I refused to even try to learn. This caused a real deprivation to Espy, when we were first married, as my inability to play bridge cut us out of all social affairs, except dances. He hated missing the gay parties he was used to. But I still think that he suffered less from his enforced absence from them than he would have suffered from my complete lack of card sense and competitive instinct, had I yielded to his urging and tried to learn to play bridge!

Although Espy had grown up in a country that was still full of game, he had little interest in hunting. He killed deer sometimes, but he lacked the true hunter's zeal. The only hunting he really enjoyed was bear hunting.

In his youth, black bear were still plentiful in the Davis Mountains and were a constant menace to stock. Big hunts involving many men on horseback and packs of dogs were common. Espy participated in many of these and could tell of his experiences. In the latter years of his life, his grandchildren's greatest delight was in listening to his vivid and wildly exciting tales of actual and imaginary bear hunts.

He also enjoyed panther hunting. Like bear hunting, panther hunts were not mere sport, but had a serious purpose – the killing of destructive predators.

In Espy's childhood, quail had been plentiful in this country. Espy kept traps set for them to supplement the family's diet. But he would never allow quail hunting on the ranch and protected every small covey. Coyotes, jackrabbits, and rattlesnakes were natural enemies, and these he killed at every opportunity.

One of his outstanding characteristics was a great love for animals. He liked all kinds of animals and did not enjoy killing anything except predators or rattlesnakes.

An unwritten law of the West – second only to that of shutting gates – was never to let a rattlesnake escape alive. It was almost a religion with Espy to kill every one he came across, though they were the only things I ever knew him to be afraid of. I have seen him kill many, and with every imaginable weapon – rocks, tire chains, pieces of wood or pipe, even frail stalks of cactus, but he never let one get away if he could possibly help it.

He had many pets during his life – dogs, deer, a bear cub, even a pair of antelope fawns which he found beside their dead mother. He carried the tiny things home and, with loving care, raised them on a bottle. This happened shortly before we were married, when antelopes were an almost extinct species and were rigidly protected by law. It was illegal to keep one in your possession. Knowing this, Espy wrote the State Game Commission and asked for permission to keep this pair he had saved.

As a poor reward for his honesty, for they would never have known that he had the little antelope had he not asked to be allowed to keep them, not only did two game wardens appear promptly and take away his pets, but they fined him $25 in the bargain!

During those years following his return from the Navy, and before his marriage, Espy had three nearly fatal illnesses. The first was an acute attack of appendicitis. He was rushed to El Paso by train, but the appendix ruptured on the way. Dr. Ramey, a famous surgeon of that time, operated on him immediately following his arrival in El Paso and saved his life, though he lay in the hospital for three weeks afterwards with a drain tube in his side.

But he was young and vigorous and soon recovered so thoroughly that he was back in a short time at the strenuous duties of a cowhand – with the result that, exactly a year later, he had to go back to El Paso for a hernia operation. This experience taught him to be more careful of his health and from then on he had no further trouble from the rupture.

The following year there occurred one of those periods of desperate crisis so common in the ranch business. Mr. Joe had gone off, buying and selling as always, and had left Espy in charge of a bunch of starving cattle. Drought and bad weather and lack of water worsened their predicament. Espy was unable to reach Mr. Joe to get help or feed.

When water and food finally became available to the poor animals which he had been trying so frantically to keep alive, Espy collapsed from the strain and was dangerously ill for weeks. He lay in a coma at the old hotel, and the doctor who was then living in Ft. Davis pronounced his illness encephalitis.

I have often wondered if it might not have been a complete nervous breakdown, brought on by overwork and worry. Espy had the cattleman's love for livestock and deep concern for their welfare. He was always extremely sympathetic with their suffering, so much so that I have accused him at times of having more sympathy for cattle than for humans! Whatever his illness was, he made a complete recovery after a few weeks, and was left with no ill effects.

During these years, he virtually lived in the saddle, as he looked after Mr. Joe's widespread herds. Long cattle drives were part of the routine life, as this was before the days of "truckers" or good roads. Espy was accustomed to driving all the cattle that were sold on the ranches to the railroad – often distances of sixty or seventy miles and across mountainous country.

Like any other working cowpuncher, he had many falls and many close brushes with danger – usually he had Mexicans working under him. At one period he was in camp for six weeks with a Mexican fence building crew and did not hear a word of English. He perfected his Spanish then, learning to speak it fluently though ungrammatically.

I often told Espy that his other great mistake in life – second only to going back to work for Mr. Joe on his return from the Navy – was in not getting married during those years. It was not from lack of opportunity, for Espy liked the ladies, and courted many of the girls in the area.

Again, lack of nerve restrained him, for his mother preached to him incessantly that he couldn't afford to marry. This was entirely true. Cowpunchers couldn't and, at an earlier date, didn't!

But if Espy had married one of the girls he went with during those years and had left his Uncle Joe and struck out for himself, he would have been a happier and richer man. His long hours and heavy responsibilities on the ranches left him with little leisure to repine however, and he was still young enough to "clean up" after work and ride a horse to see a girl or attend a dance at every opportunity.

In 1921, Espy had a chance to purchase a small ranch southwest of Ft. Davis, called "The Grierson Place". It had recently been part of the Andrew Prude ranch, when Mr. Jessie Merrill purchased the Prude Ranch, he did not want this part of it, which was cut off from the main ranch. He encouraged Espy to buy it and loaned him the money to pay for it.

It consisted of four sections of very rough, mountainous country, and was incapable of expansion, because it was surrounded by larger ranches. But it was *Land*, and land rarely came on the market in Jeff Davis County at that time. So Espy bought it, and by means of rigid economy and good management of his small herd of stock, was able to pay for it by 1925. Mr. Joe encouraged Espy to buy the Grierson, as usual for a reason. He could not buy the land himself from Mr. Merrill, but he figured that Espy would be unable to pay for it, so would eventually be forced to sell to him.

Mrs. Miller, Mr. Miller, Audrey, Espy with car in front of Limpia Hotel in Fort Davis, Texas, sometime early 1920's. (Mr. Brawe (?) & Sally Crockett on the porch.)

Meanwhile, Espy's brother, Keesey, went to A&M College in 1919 and graduated there in Mechanical Engineering in 1924. Over the years the Union Trading Company had prospered and expanded, and now also owned the Fort Davis State Bank and the Limpia Hotel. Many different persons had managed the hotel temporarily and unsuccessfully, though the tourist patronage was heavy in those years.

Finally in 1922, Mr. Miller, disgusted with a succession of incompetent managers, moved his family from their home to the hotel, and took over the management himself. Neither he nor his wife had had any experience in hotel keeping, though Mrs. Miller's father, Henry Clay Espy, had run an old hotel in San Saba in her childhood.

The hotel did a brisk business in summer visitors "summer swallows," Mr. Miller called them. He added a large dining room to the hotel and later built an "annex" of 25 rooms across the street. He hired cooks and housemaids, whom Mrs. Miller supervised. Her imperious ways and extreme penuriousness resulted in a constant fluctuating staff, and it required both unrelenting hard work and much diplomacy on Mr. Millers's part to keep the hotel running.

Espy was still working for Mr. Joe and living at the Red Barn – a mile south of town. He had by now acquired a Model T Ford, and would often drive into the hotel after work, for a good meal or to spend the night.

+

In August 1923, late one afternoon, a party of four ladies from Austin drove up to the hotel in a Model T. Ford. This created quite a local sensation, as this was the first group of women to have made

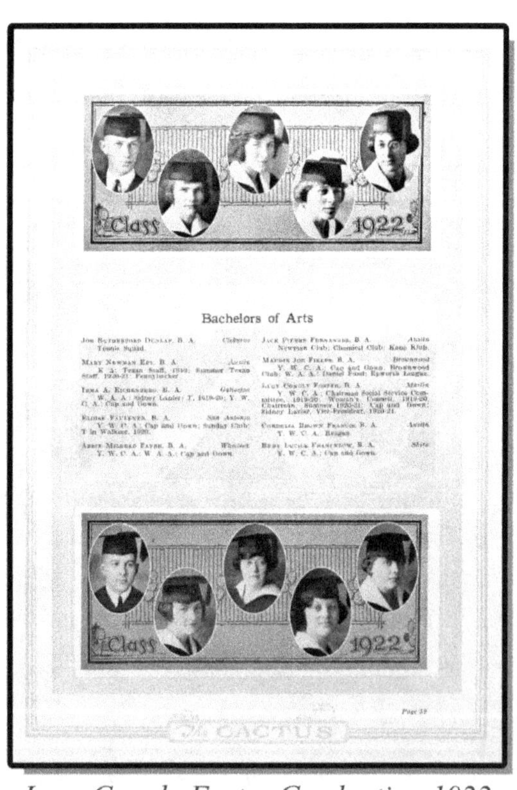

Lucy Conoly Foster Graduation 1922

the long overland trip – five days – from Austin to Fort Davis. The ladies were my mother, Mrs. Albert H. Foster, and two friends, Mrs. T.J. Broad and Miss Sallie Crocket and me – Lucy Conoly Foster, twenty-one years old, Extension Specialist in History and Economics of the Package Loan Library of the University of Texas, and owner of the Ford. It had been recently purchased for $600 out of my munificent salary of $125 monthly.

The weather was delightfully cool, the mountain scenery was a surprise and pleasure to Central Texans, so we decided to stay on at the hotel for a few days.

Lucy Conoly Foster as a young woman

My objective on the trip was El Paso, where I was to meet my fiancée, Paul Gardenere, who was then playing professional baseball in Pategonia, Arizona. But a letter came from Paul soon after our arrival in Ft. Davis, explaining his inability to keep our appointment in El Paso because of a conflict with his professional engagements.

We were both mature people and well aware of the danger of marrying a stranger. I was an ambitious emancipated feminist, quite confident of my ability to set the world on fire (at *what* I had not quite decided!), but my plans certainly did not include marriage to a poor cowpuncher.

Espy was literally scared to death of marriage and thoroughly convinced of his mother's oft-repeated warning that he could not support a wife. Besides, his own good sense warned him that I was no suitable wife for a cowpuncher. But, in spite of all our reservations, we were married July 18, 1925 in the living room of our Austin home at 1908 University Ave. in the presence of about forty-five of my friends and relatives. Poor Espy was all alone – not even a best man to support him! Looking back, I wonder that he did not break and run away.

He had borrowed his father's Dodge Sedan for the trip to Austin, but with characteristic close-mouthness, had not told his family that he was going to be married. Neither had he told a friend, Randy Casner, who had made the trip from Alpine to San Antonio with him. We met Mr. Casner in San Antonio two or three days later and, when Espy introduced me as his wife, the poor man was dumbfounded.

When Espy arrived in Austin the night before our wedding, he pulled out a handful of diamond and platinum wedding bands from his pocket and told me to chose one. I knew his limited means, so chose the one with the fewest diamonds. We went to the Robert E. Lee Hotel in San Antonio for our honeymoon. When we went to the jewelry store the next day to return the rings and pay for mine, I was astonished to learn that the jeweler had allowed Espy, a complete stranger to him, to carry off the whole lot of rings with no security whatsoever. This was my first experience of a trait of Espy's that I was to see frequent instances of in the coming years – his ability to bluff his way through any situation.

The honeymoon was marred for him by a sudden and violent toothache, necessitating a visit to a dentist and the removal of an abscessed tooth. The dentist was perhaps inexpert, for he left pieces of the broken tooth in the jaw to ache and fester. We stopped next day in Junction for a visit with my cousin, Mamie Kessee Cowsart, and her family. The following day in Ozona, Espy was suffering so with toothache that we had to hunt up another dentist – a good one this time, who was able to relieve him.

News of our wedding had preceded us to Ft. Davis. When we walked into the hotel, Mr. Miller welcomed me with the courtesy and warmth he always showed me, and the timid little sister, Audrey, greeted me with shy friendliness. But Mrs. Miller was bitterly displeased over the unexpected marriage of her favorite son and told me flatly that she didn't see how Espy expected to support a wife! I didn't either, but naively supposed that was his concern.

We began housekeeping in the Miller's old home which happened not to be rented at the time. Each evening, at Mr. Miller's insistence, we went to the hotel for our evening meal with them. This did not add to Mrs. Miller's work, as the hotel had a good Mexican cook, Juana. I learned to my astonishment, that Espy had no job. He had quit work for his Uncle Joe before he left to be married. I have always felt that Mr. Joe blamed me for the loss of the best hand he ever had, but I was completely innocent of the charge.

+

Within a month of our marriage, Mr. C.O. Finley came to Espy and offered to sell him part of the Holland Ranch, the lower portion of which was known as the Buford. There were eight sections in this ranch and the price was $8 an acre ($40,960). Mr. Finley was in financial difficulties and was about to lose his home ranch in the Davis Mountains, so was willing to sacrifice part of the more recently acquired Holland Ranch.

As long as I live, I shall never forget the terrible uncertainty and anxiety Espy underwent in the next few days – trying to make the agonizing decision of whether to undertake the staggering load of debt buying this ranch would entail. He could not sleep at night for worrying about the problem. Hour after hour I could feel his fingers nervously drumming on my shoulder – an involuntary habit I learned to know well - as he tried to decide whether to take the plunge and saddle himself for the rest of his life with a heavy load of debt.

It was not easy to borrow money then. Espy had first borrowed money from the town barber and usurer, Nick Mersfelder, at a ruinous 13%. A ranch could not pay back that rate of interest.

Espy had a friend, Al Driffel, a former mining engineer, who offered to loan him money at a more reasonable rate. So, with this help and his father's encouragement, he finally decided to undertake the tremendous gamble of buying a ranch.

I do not know exactly when or where Espy met Al Driffel, but it was probably through his Uncle Joe Espy. One of Mr. Joe's many business partners over the years had been George Gleim, an educated man from the North, who, with his brother, E.M. Gleim, had become wealthy thru a mercantile business in the then thriving mining town of Shafter.

George Gleim had married a Mexican woman, by whom he had three children, Fidel, Victoria, and Mercedes.[10] Mercedes married Al Driffel, a young mining engineer who managed Mr. Gleim's interests in the quicksilver mine at Terlingua. I found a letter to Espy, written in 1919, on stationery which bears the imprint "Big Bend Cinnabar Co., J.W. Espy, Pres., Al Driffel, Secretary.

10 "Mercedes was E.M. Gleim's daughter." Lucy Miller Jacobson

Joe Espy and George Gleim were also partners in the Ryan Ranch. Mercedes inherited considerable money from her father, who was dead by then, and it was part of this money that Espy borrowed from Al Driffel at 10%.

He sold the Grierson Ranch to Mr. Joe at this time and used that money to make the down payment on the Holland Ranch, while the money borrowed from Al Driffel was used to buy cattle to stock it, and for many other things necessary to starting a new ranch.

The first necessity was to build a division fence between the Buford and the rest of the Holland Ranch, so that Espy's cattle would not stray into Mr. Finley's pastures. He bought wire and posts, hired two Mexicans, and carried all of this, along with his camp equipment and a little food to the Holland Ranch in his open Model T Ford – the only vehicle he owned.

The two largest of the officer's houses at Camp Holland were used by Mr. Finley's family as a summer home, but he allowed Espy to camp in the third house which was vacant. It had, as I recall, a dilapidated stove in the kitchen and a pair of rusty bedsprings in one room – no water, plumbing, lights or shades.

Camp Holland, image courtesy of Miller Family

Espy doubtless figured that he had better begin breaking in his tenderfoot wife to the realities of ranch life early, so he took me along on this fence-building expedition. I was too cowardly to stay alone in the

First Homestead for Daughter and Espy, Camp Holland,
image courtesy of Beth Francell

isolated canyon, and had nothing to do there anyway, so every morning, after getting an early breakfast and packing a lunch, I would go with the men down into the flat where the fence was being built and sit all day in the car.

Espy had the typical Western ideas that a wife would share all her husband's burdens. I had been brought up among Southern men, whose attitude was that women should be shielded and protected from hardship whenever possible. He had hoped that I might employ myself usefully by cleaning the dirt out of the freshly dug post holes with a tin can, but he was soon disillusioned. I had no aptitude for doing a man's job – nor any desire to learn.

So I occupied the day during the three long weeks on this job with reading, embroidery and letter writing – and staring at the harsh, unfamiliar mountain and desert landscape, and wondering about this stranger I had married and this completely alien life I had begun.

In later years, Espy always claimed that I sat in the car and cried all day, and he invariably added that he couldn't imagine why I was crying, because we had every comfort in the world we needed – a roof over our heads, a cookstove and a pair of bed springs!

When the fence building was completed, the next job was to move Espy's cattle from Ft. Davis to the Buford – a distance of nearly sixty miles. He owned a small herd of cattle at the Grierson, and bought another bunch from Mr. Jessie Fisher. He also owned half a dozen horses and a gray mule named Rat.

His favorite horse was Eagle, a big, powerful white horse, so ill-tempered and dangerous that nobody but Espy would get on him. I once heard Frank Jones, no mean horseman himself, say that he wouldn't get on Eagle for $1,000! Espy himself had plenty of respect for Eagle's temper, and would often say to me, as he started off on the snorting and "bumping" horse, "Mama, this horse is going to kill me some day."

But Eagle never did, nor even hurt Espy. He possessed tremendous strength and Espy rode him longer than any other horse he ever owned and had a real affection for him, in spite of his bad disposition. He, on Eagle, and a Mexican on Rat drove the herd of cattle across country to their new home. I did not go along this time, as Espy had already learned, after a disastrous attempt to teach me at the Grierson place, that I couldn't ride a horse.

Lucy Conoly Foster, July, 1906 - Seven Falls,
Colorado Springs, Colorado

1925 had been a good, wet year, and that September all the Holland Ranch was covered with a beautiful stand of gamma grass, knee high and "headed out" in fat black heads. Mr. Finley hated to part with the country, for he said that in all the years he had known it, he had never seen it "look as good" as it did that fall. The Buford had one windmill, with a rock storage tank for water and troughs for the cattle to drink from. Espy's cattle were in paradise that fall, and he had achieved a lifetime ambition – to own the Holland Ranch, or part of it.

During that first fall we continued living in the Miller house in Ft. Davis, while Espy went back and forth frequently to look after his cattle there at Buford. There was no house on the place, so we could not live there, but, with plenty of grass and water, the cattle were thriving.

My mother came out from Austin for a visit that fall, bringing many of her pretty things to make my new home more livable. At Christmas time, Espy and I went to Marlin to the annual reunion of the Conoly and Bartlett families, held in the home of my Uncle Zenas and Aunt Mamie Bartlett. Their eldest son, Conoly Bartlett was married to Katharine ("Tena") Beard that Christmas, and I sang *Dawning* at the wedding, clad in my own skin-tight, above the knee length beige satin wedding dress.

On our return West, Mother decided to come with us – a disastrous decision for her and for us. She was quite happily situated in Austin, with many friends and interests, and an independent living from renting our old home at 1908 University Avenue and from the residue of my father's estate. But she could not endure being separated from her only child, and she felt that I needed her – especially now that I was pregnant with my first child.

In our part of the country, it had always been customary for widows to live with their married daughters. Grandmother Conoly lived with Uncle Zenus and Aunt Mamie for the last thirty years of her life, and at her death, her son-in-law said that she "had been a benediction in my home always!" So, mother had plenty of precedent to justify her move.

At that time, she was still a young and pretty woman, witty and charming and almost a genius musically. She could have had a good life in Austin as many of her friends did. Instead, she chose to spend the rest of her life in a country she hated and where she always felt herself an alien, out of a mistaken sense of duty to "Daughter". Her psychopathic jealousy of Espy was, for thirty years, the greatest problem of our marriage.

Looking back, it is a miracle to me that the marriage survived those first few years. Had Espy and I belonged to different nationalities, we could not have been more different than we were.

As a matter of fact, we were of different nationality. He was a Westerner, the descendant of generations of pioneering ancestors, and was himself a survivor from the pioneer era. I was a Southerner, from a part of Texas directly descended from the Old South, and my pioneering ancestors had been too far back for me to have any recollection of them.

We were both mature people, he 29 and I 23, both headstrong and high strung, and both thoroughly "sot" in our ways. Not only were our backgrounds different, but we were different in practically every other way, and had almost diametrically opposed ideas on every subject under the sun.

From his long years of "batching" and from precepts of his domineering mother, from the example of his Aunt Lola Espy, who was the perfect ranch wife, and from the unwholesome advice of two cynical, woman hating friends, Nick Mersfelder and Edwin Fowlkes, Espy had formed a rigid idea of what he expected in a wife.

I did not fit that idea, and neither did I want to. I considered myself a sophisticated, intellectual and emancipated woman, and no man was going to run over me – no matter what black looks he gave me when I displeased him – which was often!

Over the years we had almost every kind of marital trouble – financial, religious, in-laws, disagreements over the raising of our children, - everything except infidelity, for somehow, in spite of all our disagreements and quarrels, we never fell out of love with each other.

Attempting to run a ranch from a distance of sixty miles soon became too much of a burden, both physically and financially, for Espy. He got permission from Mr. Finley for us to live in the officer's house at Camp Holland where we had camped during the fence building the previous fall.

Soon after January 1st, we moved all our possessions from Ft. Davis to Camp Holland. These consisted of our wedding presents, part of Mother's old furniture (only part of it would go into the four tiny rooms of our new house), Espy's bachelor gear and some furniture he inherited from his Miller grandparents. Mr. Miller helped us move.

Kind Mr. Miller always helped us with everything, but Mrs. Miller's continuing cruelty to me, whom she considered the worst wife Espy could possibly have chosen – and told me so! – made me thankful to get away from Ft. Davis. My mother accompanied us on the move. We woke up in our new home that first morning to find that a heavy snow had fallen in the night. In the snow were tracks of some large wild animal encircling the house. Mother and I felt that we had come to the end of the world.

Meanwhile Espy, who was always a competent "handy man" set about making us more comfortable. He connected our house to Mr. Finley's water tank and installed a sink and second-hand bathtub in the house. The flush toilets were in separate small buildings at the rear of each house. Eventually he connected us with Mr. Finley's Delco system, so that we could put aside the Kerosene lamps.[11]

We cleaned and patched and Kalsomined [12] the little house, and Mother, who had a real talent for making a home attractive soon had it livable with her old things.

Espy was working furiously. There was so much to do and so little to do with, but he was busy constantly with repairs inside and chores outside the house. He made many trips back and forth to Ft. Davis for necessities and supplies, but Mother and I did not leave the Holland Camp from the day we moved there in January until we went to Valentine in June and took the train to Marlin for Clay to be born.

We had numerous visitors. Unexpected visitors were another Western Custom I had to get used to. The Millers came often from Ft. Davis, and good Mr. Miller always saw what we were most in need of and tried to bring it to us.

I recall a remark of Mrs. Miller's on her first visit to us, when she noticed the Finley cows standing around our house (for there was no fence to keep them away), "Don't you just *love* cows? They're so much company!" I hope that I did not show my disgust, for already I hated cows.

11 In 1916 the Delco Light Company introduced a generator and battery system to serve isolated locations. This was two decades before the New Deal Rural Electrical Administration (1935), brought power to much of America. By 1929 Delco was producing over 300,000 units a year, and one of those was in service at the Miller Ranch. A wind driven propeller operated a generator that charged several glass jar batteries that could produce as much as 750 watts of power, enough for several light bulbs and a small appliance or two.
12 "Kalsomined" is the application of whitewash, slaked lime and chalk, used as a form of cheap white paint.

Neighboring cowpunchers and ranchmen came to see us. I imagine there was some curiosity about Espy's city bride. Dear Mr. Van Neal and his wife, who were our closest neighbors and who were to become life-long friends, came often. Mr. Conring, owner of the old Valentine Trading Co., which Mr. Keesey had established, George Newton, Mrs. Miller's first cousin, Mr. John Means, Mr. Sam Bunton and others visited us.

It was Mr. Means and Mr. Van Neal who told us the story of the Massacre of the Negro Soldiers there on Vieja Mesa.[13] Mr. Means was a great tease, he asked me if I wasn't scared of the ghosts of the Negro soldiers, and I replied, scornfully, that I wasn't scared of anything dead! But there were plenty of live things to be scared of; bulls (for I had not yet learned the mild nature of Hereford bulls), rattlesnakes, and the sinister looking Mexicans who were constantly crossing the Vieja trail across the canyon from our house. They looked like bandits to me, with their burros heavily laden with wicker panniers. I have often heard blood curdling stories of the Brite raid, which had happened less than ten years earlier and less than twenty miles away, and many other stories of border raids and murders. This was in the days of Prohibition, and the Mexicans were probably tequila smugglers, and were as scared of me, no doubt, as I was of them.

Two more lonely and miserable women than Mother and me were during those months would have been hard to find. The memory of that terrible first year I would gladly erase from my mind. What Espy thought is something else again. With Mother constantly in close proximity, we had little chance to exchange confidences or work out our frequent misunderstandings. After I knew him better, and came to appreciate how difficult the situation was for him, I marveled that he endured it with the grace he did.

There was one bright spot in those months. Late one afternoon in early spring, Espy looked out to see a car drive up and observed, "Here comes Uncle Judge and his new bride." His Uncle Judge (Robert Henry Espy) had married Buelah Durrell of Van Horn the previous December. Judge was only eight years older than Espy, and though they were very

13 On June 11, 1880, Lieutenant Frank Mills and a detachment of Pueblo Scouts were camping in Vieja Pass when shortly after sunrise they were attacked by a band of Apache. The Indians were driven off, but Simon Olgin, head of the scouts and a Pueblo Chief was killed.

different in many ways, the two had always been – and always remained – more like brothers than like uncle and nephew.

Judge was the younger brother of Joe Espy. No two brothers were ever more different. Joe Espy was one of the worst men I ever knew, and Judge Espy was one of the best. I was instantly indignant at these arriving guests. The very idea of them coming in on me, in my embarrassing condition, uninvited and unannounced! They came in and spent the weekend with us, and from that day forward were loyal and devoted friends for the rest of our lives.

In June Mother and I went back to Marlin on the train, for my baby was due early in July. On July 5th Espy also arrived in Marlin, having won a lucky bet at the July 4th Rodeo in Alpine that provided him with funds for the trip!

Our son, Clay Espy Miller, Jr., was born at 7^{AM} on July 7th at the Allen Hospital, with my cousin's husband and my good friend, Dr. Milton Davison, officiating. My first awareness of the event was of Espy, jumping wildly up and down, and calling to me, "Mama, it's a boy!" His joy and pride in the little black haired fellow was inordinate and his love for him instantaneous. He returned soon after to the ranch, but I stayed on at the Bartletts for a month, recovering my strength, and getting used to the care of a little newcomer.

Immediately after Espy's return to the ranch, Mr. Finley came to him again and offered to sell him the remainder of the Holland Ranch – still at the $8 price. This time there was no hesitation on Espy's part. He had a ranch, a wife and a son – he could conquer the world!

He accepted Mr. Finley's offer at once, and the necessary loans and legal matters were attended to. He borrowed money again from Al Driffel for this purchase. He bought all the land remaining in the Old Holland Ranch (5,732 acres at $8.00 per acre) and all the cattle on the ranch (309 head) and five mules – a total debt of $45, 385.

In August Mother, Clay and I returned to Valentine on the train, and went back up into the Holland Camp. Mr. Finley soon moved the family of his tenant farmer, Lewis Hickman, from the old Holland Ranch house in the flat.

Now that that house was empty, we immediately decided that it was a more desirable place to live than the camp, and on October 22, 1926, we moved into it.

Mr. Finley had made the house over some years earlier for the use of his daughter and son-in-law, Zora and Nat Gunter, but they had later moved to South Texas and had completely denuded the house, even the bathroom fixtures and the kitchen sink!

The house was now in a shocking state of repairs, in spite of poor Mrs. Hickman's best efforts to keep it, for Lewis Hickman was a shiftless cowpuncher who would not even chop wood for the fireplace, but burned long limbs which lay out on the floor. As a result, the living room floor was covered with burned spots. The "bead" ceiling was studded with bullet holes – where old John Holland, on his habitual sprees, had used it for target practice!

Espy hired a fellow cowpuncher and friend, Charlie Nunn, to help him with the move. They first cleaned the worst of the dirt out of the house. I recall that Charlie put out rat poison in the milkhouse one night and next morning carried out 14 dead rats!

Mr. Miller secured from somewhere a second-hand sink and bathroom fixtures and these Espy, working alone and with intense concentration, installed to fit the pipes already in the house. He did this so expertly that I was fond of telling him afterwards that if we "went broke" (a constant threat to ranchmen) and lost the ranch, he could always make a living as a plumber!

He patched the worst holes in the plaster inside the house and with my help (for I was learning what was expected of a ranchman's wife) Kalsomined the whole interior in a soft cream color.

The greatest improvement he made in the dark old house was in putting a skylight in the shed roof of the kitchen, thus transforming it into a bright and sunny room. He also repaired the worst leaks in the roof.

Only the most urgent repairs were made on the house, as there was also much ranch work to be done. The most essential of these was to put back into service the pipeline, which carried water from the rock tank at the mouth of ZH canyon to the house. When this was completed, we moved down into the old ranch house.

In mid-September, both my grandmothers, Mrs. Albert Ware Foster and Mrs. William Silas Conoly of Marlin, came out for a visit and entered enthusiastically into helping us get established in our new home. We all worked hard at whatever had to be done, and soon, with the installation of Mother's old furniture, made the shabby old house into an attractive and comfortable home.

Grandmother Conoly had a heart condition, and the high altitude gave her heart flurries, so, after a few weeks, she returned to Marlin, but Grandmother Foster stayed longer. She dearly loved babies, and immediately assumed charge of my tiny fretful baby.

He was starving from my misguided efforts to nurse him, and required constant attention. This freed Mother and me for cleaning and repairing jobs, as well as for the regular chores of cooking, washing, care of milk, etc. We were all working frantically, in an effort to get the house livable before bad weather set in.

A wood stove in the kitchen and a fireplace in the living room provided the only heat. Espy had grown up in the desert where wood was scarce or non-existent, and he was amazed and horrified at the amount of wood I used.

I had come from a part of the country where wood had been almost as plentiful as water, and where there were also plenty of Negroes to cut it. Thus my lavish (to Espy) use of wood became one of our continuing areas of disagreement, which did not cease until the arrival of butane gas many years later.

Grandmother was even more extravagant with wood than I was, being old and cold natured, so keeping wood hauled from the canyons and chopped to the proper size constituted one of the regular chores for Espy and a procession of hired men.

Espy had bought the Delco plant from Mr. Finley, and with the help of his brother Keesey, and his friend, Kenneth Stewart, had wired the house. With constant care of the batteries, this system provided us with lights most of the time, but it was too weak even to run an electric iron. He also repaired the phone line to Valentine, which worked intermittently.

He bought a Jersey cow, and, though he generally managed to delegate the chore of milking to his ranch helpers (his alibi was that milking was "to darn perpetual!"), I was then initiated into the equally perpetual chore of caring for the milk and butter. In this I was instructed by Mother and Grandmother, who were experts at making fine butter.

I learned to manage the old cement trough in the milk house, which Mr. Finley had built, a long, shallow trough, provided with a hydrant and drain, which had to be emptied and scrubbed with a stiff brush every morning to prevent the forming of scum and odor. For many years, this was the only refrigeration we had. Cans and bottles of perishables sat in the shallow water at one end of the trough, while a tin "milk cooler" of three shelves, the top one holding water, sitting on legs in the trough and covered with a large white cloth (which had to be changed and washed daily), sat in the lower end, between two open windows.

Milk in four-pound coffee cans was kept in this cooler, and butter, cheese and left over foods. Cleaning this cooler every morning and washing the numerous buckets and cloths was one of my most "perpetual" and time consuming jobs, but it was necessary for the health of the family.

In summer time, in spite of the care I took, the mornings milk would be sour by supper time and the butter soft. During the frequent dust storms the country was subject to, these wet milk cloths would become gray with dirt. I would often sweep dirt out of the drafty old milk house by the shovelful.

The cloths for the cooler were made of heavy cake sacks, which had been ripped and sewed together to make a straight piece about three yards long, and they were hung around the milk cooler with the aid of clothes pins. When wet and full of dirt they weighed heavily and were awkward to wash and to hang out to dry, but this was one of my regular jobs. I did the milk cloths, all the washing for the baby, as well as our underclothes, and best things at the kitchen sink, but the heavy washing – sheets, towels, Espy's dirty work-clothes - was done by wash women either in Valentine or living on the ranch.

Espy had a passion for all sorts of livestock, and we soon acquired ducks, guineas and turkeys, in addition to a large flock of chickens. I had a total lack of interest in these and refused, point blank, to take care of them, as any ranchwoman was supposed to, so their care fell to the hired hands.

I also steadfastly refused to learn to milk a cow, though that was considered woman's work in the West, because I had a strong suspicion that, if I ever learned, I would have to do it regularly!

The endless tasks incidental to establishing a ranch required help and over the years Espy had a succession of "hands," both Mexican and Whites.

Part of the code of the West, which irritated me continually, was that the man of the house was entitled to help with whatever he was doing, but the woman was not! Mrs. Miller never lacked for servants at the hotel (though her unreasonable demands on them kept poor Mr. Miller constantly searching for new ones) but she told me sternly, soon after my marriage, that "we don't have servants out here!"

This was, even then, untrue, as most of the women of my age in Ft. Davis had part- or full-time help, but Mrs. Miller did not want Espy to have that extra expense. She even resented my having the family washing done. Where I came from, no white woman I had ever known did the family washing, not even the poorest ones, there were too many Negroes for that!

I resented being expected to do this huge washing, when I already had more to do than I could possibly accomplish, but it was a source of humiliation to Espy that I didn't do it, since his mother and his Aunt Lola had in their early years. So the family washing provided another source of disagreement.

In this case, however, my determination proved stronger than Espy's for I never did do the family washing, and I promptly returned all of the three washing machines he hopefully bought for me in later years! In this stand I had the firm backing of loyal Grandmother Foster. Though she had slaved all her life for a worthless husband and had supported her family by "taking in boarders" and sewing, she was determined that I should not do certain things which she considered beneath a lady. She told me forcefully, "Daughter, don't you *ever* do this big washing! As long as Espy Miller can afford help for everything he does, he can afford to pay for a wash woman for you!" I have abided by grandmother's advice. [14]

Charlie Nunn was the first of the hired help, but he was only temporarily out of a job and was too expensive for Espy to employ permanently. He was followed by a succession of Mexicans and by much part-time help from various white men in Valentine. Mr. Miller

14 This held true until the summer of 1968, when Daughter's first great-grandchild was born. She finally broke down and purchased a washing machine so her granddaughter Beth could wash diapers.

was frequently at the ranch to "help out", and so was Espy's brother Keesey, after his graduation from A&M College and his purchase of the Ft. Davis Auto Co. from Kenneth Stewart.

When there was any big job of ranch work to be done, such as "rounding up," branding, or shipping, the custom of those days was for the ranch owner to call on all of his neighbors for help. This they did willingly, as Espy helped them in return.

There was always more help than was needed on these works, and I soon began to suspect that it was because our neighbors enjoyed the good meals they got at our house.

It was part of my job to feed the help – both paid and unpaid. White cowpunchers, however dissolute or dirty, ate with the family, but Mexican help was always served later and separately. To the day of his death, Espy could never overcome his early training in segregation enough to sit down at the table with a Mexican!

Our neighbors, the Van Neills, Clarance Bells, Sam Buntons, Ed Hunter and others were frequent visitors, as was George Newton, Mrs. Miller's cousin. All of these men in the area and others would flock in when there was the excuse of work – and sometimes without that excuse.

Espy loved good food and had rarely had it during his bleak "batching" years. So I learned early that one of the few ways I could please him was by cooking. Grandmother had been a famous cook, and though I had not had much experience in cooking before my marriage, other than making cakes and candy, with her instruction and Espy's encouragement, I soon learned. Good food was still somewhat of a rarity in those years, so we had plenty of willing male help.

Those visiting cowpunchers had a habit of squatting around my kitchen, smoking, while I prepared meals, which infuriated me. Where I came from, men never thought of entering the kitchen, which was considered the domain of women and Negroes. The presence of these idle and (I suspected) critical spectators of my work filled me with rage. I fumed in silence at these cowpunchers, Espy included, who cluttered my small kitchen and interfered with my work. I could cheerfully have brained anyone of them with a stick of stove wood!

The Western custom of feeding every one who came to your door was another that I had a hard time getting used to. We had always had lots of company in my home, but it was invited company, and the sight of a large group of people driving up unexpectedly for meals never failed to disconcert me.

+

As fall advanced, a sick baby was added to my troubles. Since I had been an only child, I was completely ignorant of child care, and Mother was not much more experienced, as my two grandmothers had largely raised me. Clay was fretful and cried incessantly and did not gain weight as my guide, Holt's *Care and Feeding of Children*, said he should.

I wrote frequently to Dr. Milton Davison for advice, but he urged me to continue nursing the baby, and felt that he would eventually start to gain. The result was that my poor baby starved! The old railroad doctor in Valentine, Dr. B.F. Vick, was no help. When I would in desperation go to him with the sick child, his invariable query was, "Well, now, Mrs. Miller, what do *you* think is the matter with this child?"

By Christmas, Clay was so thin and frail that we decided it was necessary to take him back to Marlin for Dr. Milton to treat. Besides I was bitterly homesick for my sweet, loving family in Marlin and for the gay Christmas reunion at the Bartlett's that I had always been a part of.

Mother still had money left from my father's estate then, so she paid for a luxurious trip home on the Pullman. Espy stayed at the ranch, promising to come later if he could, but it turned out that he could not.

When we reached Marlin, Milton took one horrified look at the tiny emaciated child and immediately put him on a bottle and began giving him supplementary foods and medicines. The little fellow began to gain weight immediately but it was years before he fully recovered from those months of starvation. I went on a diet and brought myself down to a respectable weight, though never again back to 115!

We returned to the ranch after Christmas. When Clay was six months old, I found to my horror, that I was pregnant again. I suppose it would be hard for a young wife of this era even to conceive of my state of mind. With my prudish upbringing and my advanced ideas about the role of women, I considered myself irrevocably disgraced by having two babies within fifteen months! My mother fully shared, even encouraged, my feelings of resentment and despair at this new catastrophe which had befallen me.

These were unhappy months that followed for all of us. Times were hard and the life we lived was harder. Espy was harassed almost beyond endurance with work and worry over depression and debts, a miserable wife, a hostile mother-in-law in his home and a mother in Ft. Davis who constantly criticized everything about his wife.

Both my mother and Mrs. Miller were abnormally possessive mothers – a type all too common in their generation. Mother's jealousy of Espy and Mrs. Miller's of me reached psychopathic proportions.

Mr. Miller, bless his heart, always acted as peacemaker and did everything in his power to smooth things over and make us all happy. He urged me not to resent "the Madam's" treatment of me. Poor man, he had been a victim of it all his married life.

But, as the months wore on, I sunk deeper into depression over my complete failure to adjust to the harsh life and to this stranger I had married, whom I could neither understand nor please. I came to feel that I could not endure to spend my life in such hostile surroundings, both natural and human, and that the only solution was to end the marriage in divorce.

I know now that had we been permitted to work out our differences together, without the constant interference of both our mothers, matters would never have reached such a state between Espy and me. In spite of what he considered my incessant failures as a ranchman's wife, Espy was violently opposed to any separation. I was his wife, for better or worse, and an incurable optimist that he was, he always hoped to turn me into the kind of wife he thought he wanted. But I was too wretched, physically and mentally, to try any longer, so in September 1927, Mother, Clay, and I, went back to Marlin, moving her furniture back with us.

We settled in a little upstairs apartment at Grandmother Foster's, and there on October 17, our daughter, Betty, was born. She was named Mary Elizabeth for my two aunts, Mary Conoly Bartlett and Bess Conoly Bradford.

It was wonderful for me to be back in the midst of my devoted relatives, who poured out all their love and concern on "Daughter" and her babies.[15] My father's brother, Dr. Willett Foster, sweetest and best of

---

15 Lucy was named for her mother, and in a southern tradition was called "Daughter," a name continued by her grandchildren and great-grandchildren.

men, adored little Clay and was, in practice, his doting grandfather. Grandmother Foster idolized Betty from the day of her birth.

In a warm, close and highly articulate family like mine, my marital problems were under frequent discussion. The women felt almost unanimously that the situation was impossible to continue. But the men felt differently. My Uncle Willett, Uncle Harry Conoly and Uncle Zenas Bartlett all liked Espy, and they all realized that the real trouble with my marriage was Mother. They urged me to return to Espy.

Meanwhile Espy had been writing me constantly, begging me to come back, and at Christmas, came in person. He made the long drive from Ft. Davis to Marlin in 18 hours of straight driving – a sort of record for that time. It did not take Espy and me long to realize that our love was greater than our disagreements.

We both knew that Mother was the greatest cause of our difficulties, and he tried his best to persuade me not to let her return West with us. But I was still too much under Mother's domination, and too thoroughly instilled with my duty as a daughter, so, in spite of Espy's pleading and of the sensible advice of my uncles, I insisted that Mother would have to come back too.

Espy loved me enough to agree, but my mistaken sense of filial duty to my mother resulted in thirty years of difficulty for our marriage and of constantly increasing unhappiness for her.

We came back to Valentine after Christmas, bringing the much-traveled furniture with us, and settled down to life at the ranch. With all our problems unresolved.

Both Espy and I were shaken by the experience, for we had learned from it how much we meant to each other, in spite of our disagreements. Never again was there to be any consideration of a separation. We were both determined to make a success of our marriage, no matter how tough the going.

The disagreements never ceased, and new and different ones were added as years went by, but we began to realize that our first loyalty was to each other, not to our warring mothers. Also we were united by our children, as their care and development became our primary concern.

Meanwhile work on the ranch was increasing. The place had poor outhouses, two bug-infested shanties for Mexicans, a dilapidated chicken house, a few corrals and an old garage. Both the Mexican houses and the garage were to burn in the years ahead, and to be replaced with more substantial structures. Espy tore down the big wooden barns at Camp Holland, and moved the lumber down to the ranch house.

In the winter of 1928, he began erecting the big red barn and adjoining corrals from these materials. This labor occupied many months for Espy was a conscientious builder. Anything he built was built to last and it was "Hell for stout!"

Mr. Miller had given us a Farmall tractor the previous year, a useful vehicle that served us well for many years. With it Espy put in and cultivated fields of Alfalfa, which were watered from the big dirt tank at the foot of the mountains.

There was a fine orchard below this tank, which produced the largest and most delicious peaches I ever ate, along with much other fruit. There were also a few fruit trees and an old garden spot south of the house. Espy immediately began putting in a new orchard here and making a new garden nearer the house. Most of the Mexicans were good gardeners, and we always had a fine garden during the summer, regardless of rains. From these men I learned their age-old practices of irrigation, which I copied in the flower gardens I made around the house.

I think it was in the Spring of 1928 that Espy, who did most of the shopping for the family, picked up a hobo in Valentine and brought him home to work. This was a tall, thin boy from Urbana, Illinois named Jim Wardlow. He had run away from home and had drifted for several years. He was bright though poorly educated, and proved to be apt at learning ranch skills. He made us a valuable hand for a couple of years. He lived in the little back room off the porch, which we still call "Jim's room". He was faithful, agreeable and industrious and was devoted to Clay and Betty, who responded warmly. To my horror, I discovered that they soon began picking up his illiterate speech. Then one day he collected his wages and left – never to return or be heard of again.[16]

After Jim and other helpers of varying duration, Espy brought over a Mexican family from Ft. Davis. The head of the family was

---

16 Later, while Daughter was living in a nursing home in Alpine, he and his wife would visit her, according to Lucy Miller Jacobson

Piedro ("Pete") Viesca, with whom Espy had worked as a boy and his aged parents, his wife Manuella, and her large family (originally 14) of younger brothers and sisters. They lived in the ram-shackled old houses, and became not only faithful servants but loyal friends.

Old Elario, Pete's father, was too old for heavy work, but he would go out into the pastures in summer and gather a certain kind of green reed, from which he wove beautiful baskets for me. Pete was an expert cowhand and a hard and steady worker. Manuella, a large placid woman, as beautiful as a Madonna in her youth, mothered her orphan brood and my little ones.

Over the years, one after another of these children died, usually of the family curse of tuberculosis, though one boy, Felas, died in action in World War II, until only Manuella and Ciquel were left. Ciquel [17] was a boy in his early teens when he came to the Holland Ranch. Under Espy's expert tutorage, he developed into the most expert cowpuncher we ever had. In later years, he was top hand at the Miller Ranch.

Soon after our return from Marlin in 1928, Espy glassed in the sleeping porch on the south side of the house, and converted it into a comfortable bedroom for the babies and us. Later that year, he glassed in the back porch, which added greatly to the warmth and comfort of the house.

He had inherited a knack for using tools from his Miller forebears, and, like all the Millers, he was a fair carpenter and liked to build things. One of his first efforts, after we moved to the ranch, had been to build the shop.

This had originally been the guard house at Camp Holland on the edge of ZH canyon before he tore it down and moved it. I will always remember his dismay, the morning after he had finished putting up the framework for his new shop, when he went out and found that a high wind during the night had laid it flat on the ground! This may have been the reason for his subsequent mania for building things "stout!"

Although his chief desire was to improve the ranch premises, he was, from necessity, constantly making small repairs and improvements on the house, especially patching the roof. This was worn out when we

17 It should be noted that his name was Ezquel Gonzales; As late as May 2008, he was living alone in his home in Pecos and has some of his descendants bring him to the ranch once or twice a year – Clay Espy Miller, Jr.

moved into the house, but it was nearly 15 years before we were able to put on a new roof.

Espy had a passion for building fences, and he moved fences, I used to tell him, as often as some housewives moved furniture. He had quite an ingenious mechanical talent and loved to figure out and execute intricate fastenings on gates and other labor-saving devices.

While we were living at Holland Camp, he rigged up a long wire to the chicken house, a quarter of a mile away, so that he could open the door of the chicken house without leaving our house.

Another patent of his was a kitchen towel hung by a cord which would spring back to the ceiling when released. He quite fancied this invention and got his feelings hurt when I refused to allow a dirty towel to hang from my kitchen ceiling.

He devoted much time and ingenuity to working out latches for the many gates, with the result that almost every gate on the ranch had a different kind of fastening on it.[18] The nearest he ever came to a quarrel with Judge was once when he made fun of the extremely primitive fastenings on the gates on Judge's ranch, and Judge took offense at his criticisms.

Judge, being an Espy, was a cowpuncher but no carpenter. He was an expert at anything that he could do on a horse and inept at anything that had to be done off of one. Many years later, when I was convalescing from an operation in an El Paso hospital, Judge used to visit me faithfully. One afternoon, while reminiscing about this particular trait of Espy's, he came as near criticizing Espy as he ever did, when he confided to me his belief that "Old Espy just *improves* too much!"

The children were growing. Betty was a beautiful, healthy baby. She had never starved like poor Clay and was plump and good natured.

Clay was beginning to out grow his bad start in life. He walked at nine months, talked plainly before a year and showed an early interest in books and reading. His remarkable memory soon became noticeable. He had a favorite story book called *Willie Mouse* which he could recite

18 To experience this, just come to the front gate of the Espy Miller (Francell) Home in Fort Davis and operate the front gate.

Espy holding Clay, Daughter with Betty

verbatim and with great emphasis when very young. Espy was so proud of this feat that he always had him do it for visitors, and he preserved the well-worn little volume among his treasures.

The children had many pets and lived an active, healthy life out-of-doors, in spite of my constant terror of rattlesnakes. Clay's first dog was a little terrier Espy ordered from Minnesota, called Minnie Gump, who later died from a rattlesnake bite. Later there was an enormous, pedigreed black German Shepherd, called Midnight, who, it transpired, ate chickens, so had to be given away. Still later there was Rusty, a beautiful red Shepherd, who eventually died an agonizing death from a poisoned strychnine bait, which had been put out to kill coyotes. And there was always an adequate supply of kittens, which both children loved.

Christmas 1928 Mother, the Children and I went back to Marlin to visit, leaving Espy at the ranch. Betty was an adorable fourteen-month-old, curly haired and beautiful, and pet of the entire family.

One afternoon her proud (great) Grandmother Foster dressed her up in her best and took her up to show off to an old friend, Mrs. J.T. Robinson. Mrs. Robinson's granddaughter had been playing with her toys in the rooms, but her mother took her out before she let the visitor in, explaining that Betty Rose had been exposed to whooping cough. Our Betty played with her toys and promptly came down with whooping cough fourteen days later. Clay soon had it too. They were both quite sick for about two weeks, then got better, but were still contagious, so our doctor, Milton Davison, who was also the health officer, refused to allow us to ride home on the train.

After we had been confined in Marlin for six weeks, Espy borrowed his father's Chrysler sedan and came for us. We started back West but just out of Lampasas had an accident. This model of Chrysler had a flaw – one brake that locked when others did not. This happened when Espy put on the brakes and sent us into a dirt embankment. I was sitting on the front seat, holding Betty, whose head broke the windshield. She was only slightly cut, but the car was so badly damaged that we had to spend twenty-four hours in an old hotel in Lampasas, waiting for it to be repaired. Later the same car turned over with Mr. Miller, when he struck a deer on his way home from the ranch.

We returned the Miller's car in Ft. Davis, and proceeded to the ranch in our own open Ford. Both babies were still sick and miserable with the long drawn out whooping cough, and Mother and I both came down with the flu.

Jim Wardlow was working for us then. Mother often told afterwards of Jim's truthful answer, when she said to him one morning, as she was dragging around the kitchen trying to get breakfast (I was too sick to get out of bed), "Jim, what *do* they do on a ranch when all the women get sick?" and Jim replied instantly, "They just don't pay *no* attention to it!" We all finally recovered, and spring came, as it always does, with a renewal of life and hope, and summer and fall in their turn.

+

We spent our first Christmas at the ranch in 1929. We put up a Christmas tree, and Aunt Bess Bradford sent us a box of exquisite German ornaments from Denver, among them little horns which blew. Some of these little horns endured to ornament the last Christmas tree I ever decorated.

I was determined to make the holiday celebration as gay and happy as the ones I had always known. We spent weeks in careful preparations. We invited the Miller family, including "Mammy" Espy, Mrs. Miller's mother, who was by then living at the hotel with them, for Christmas dinner. We served the meal on the back porch, and though it was snowing outside, the porch was made warm and comfortable by a gasoline stove Mr. Miller brought over.

It was the very same stove, unless I am mistaken, which subsequently caught fire in a room occupied by two women at the hotel. We happened to be visiting there at the time. Espy heard the women's screams, ran to their room, grabbed the blazing stove and ran down the back stairs and into the back yard with it – and suffered only minor burns. This was an early example of his instinctive bravery which I was to see often in future years.

That first Christmas at the ranch, Espy put many hours of loving and careful work into building Betty a dollhouse out of an old apple box. It was a charming doll house, two stories high, with a hinged roof that opened back, and a cunning little outside staircase. He finished it carefully, inside and out, with paint and wall paper, and we found some little pieces of doll furniture for it. Two generations of our children, boys as well as girls, adored playing with this crude little doll house above all other toys.

✦

Espy was good at leatherwork, and was continually repairing the saddles and harness on the ranch, or putting new hide bottoms in a set of his grandfather's old ladder back chairs he had inherited. One of his most valued possessions was a large canvas bag of fine soft deerskin, which was sacred to certain uses. One of these was the making of a leather thong or string for various purposes – even, late in life, to hang around his neck to hold his glasses. It was always my task to hold the two pieces of deerskin evenly so that he could cut a thin, straight string with his knife. I was very poor at this task, as I was at most ranch jobs and it irritated him greatly that I did not take it seriously enough.

Although my help was always inadequate and often worse than none, he always wanted it, and always tried to get me to help him with whatever he was doing. In return, he was quite willing, often insistent, in helping me with certain of my jobs, especially in telling me how to cook – advice which I did not at all appreciate.

I remember when we were first married and I spent some of my leisure doing fancy work, how he would sometimes take the embroidery hoops from me and attempt to do the tiny stitches himself. The spectacle of the big, virile, dirty cowpuncher painfully laboring over an embroidery hoop was ludicrous to a degree! This did not bother Espy. His curiosity made him want to know how everything was done, regardless of how foreign or useless to him personally.

He tried hard to train me to be a good ranchwoman, but it was hopeless. I disliked cattle and was afraid of horses, and I hated the muck and filth of the corrals and branding pens. The smell of blood had always sickened me.

As a girl I used to cross a street to avoid passing in front of a butcher shop, but it was not very long before Espy insisted that I "help" him when he butchered. I was less than helpful at this job, and he finally gave up on it, except for those times when no one else was available to help him.

One of his regular tasks was shoeing horses. He insisted on my holding the horse by a rope while he worked, though I was scared to death to do so. He could not understand why I did not enjoy sitting on a corral fence and watching the branding, as the Espy girls had always done. He finally realized that all I was good for was to stay at home and cook for the workers, but as long as he lived his feelings were hurt when I failed to share any of his interest or to enjoy doing anything he was doing.

My passions for reading and flower growing were alien to him, but he tried to be understanding and cooperative.[19] He actually resented my reading (which I had precious little time for in those early years!) because it took my attention from him. When he learned to enjoy reading, this problem was eased. Anyway, most of my reading then was to the children, for I was anxious to foster in them my own love of books.

I discovered, soon after we moved to the ranch, that the good creek soil, unlimited water and ample supply of manure would produce wonderfully fine flowers, and I soon had a luxuriant flower garden growing in the side yard.

Espy admired this, for he had a keen appreciation of beauty. He used to say that he never failed to see three things – a fine horse, a good cow and a pretty woman! But he was also deeply sensitive to the beauties of nature and had a passionate love for his own "country" which was beautiful above all others to him.

19 For more about Daughter's Garden, see the Introduction.

His interest in my flower garden did not extend to helping with the work of it, though I was expected to help out in the vegetable garden, when necessary. But he did allow me the help of his men, when they were not busy, with the heavier tasks of hauling and spreading manure, spading up beds and mowing the lawn. He soon realized how greatly my flower garden enhanced the beauty of the place, but he always maintained that he couldn't afford to start helping me in the yard, because there was no end to it! Forty years ago, a flower garden was somewhat of a rarity on a West Texas ranch. "Mammy" thoroughly disapproved of my flowers and told me plainly that I'd do a lot better if I spent my time growing vegetables!

But I knew better, for growing flowers was not only my greatest pleasure, but it was my best safety valve. I soon learned that I could work off many of the worries and problems that constantly beset me in my yard, and that the constant tension under which we lived would lessen as I dug in the dirt.

I made flower beds while dragging a baby behind me in a two wheeled cart, and later with two little ones playing around me. It was happiness for all of us to be out of doors and the children soon learned to love growing things as I did.

Espy shared this love of growing things. His especial joy was in planting trees. He planted three orchards at the ranch during the years we lived there and innumerable pecan trees. He became an expert at grafting English walnuts onto our native black walnut trees. He devoted much time to pruning and training grape vines and to attempting to grow exotic varieties of fruits and berries.

Always he saw to it that we had good gardens, at which he and, more often, the Mexicans worked at odd times. Often these gardens produced large surpluses of corn, beans, tomatoes, squash, chili, watermelons and cantaloupes. One summer he grew fine watermelons by the wagonload.

There never seemed to be any market for this "garden stuff" in Valentine, so he often ended up by giving away most of the surplus. I learned canning and preserving, and "put up" hundreds of quarts of fruit every summer.

Some years later, Espy bought a large pressure cooker and sealer and tin cans by the hundreds. In summer when there was a good fruit crop, all the family and the help would work for days at the canning of fruit, and we would can up six- or seven-hundred quart cans of fruit, besides the preserves and jellies and grape juice I made.

Espy also planted a big patch of strawberries. The plants were bought from Old Anton Aggerman, the last surviving soldier in Ft. Davis and produced bumper crops of small, deliciously flavored berries.

He was also trying to raise chickens, turkeys, guineas and ducks, and this involved incessant warfare against "varmints". They were plentiful – polecats (or skunks), raccoons, ringtails, coyotes, foxes, snakes, owls, hawks and even mountain lions, though we did not realize that we had the latter until we got sheep.

Espy was continually trying to trap or poison the varmints that preyed on the fowls and even, in the case of coyotes, occasionally on calves. He finally succeeded in eliminating the prairie dog colonies by use of poison gas, thus ridding the ranch of that serious menace to life and limb. One of the occupational hazards of a cowpuncher was having his horse fall with him when he stepped into a prairie dog hole. The prairie dogs also destroyed acres of grass roots.

He also tried to get rid of the coyotes, which were plentiful then. After he began using pickups his .22 rifle was always slung from the roof of the pickup where it could easily be reached to shoot at any strange coyote or rabbit he might see.

Our neighbor, Sam Bunton, disapproved of killing the coyotes because it upset the balance of nature. When most of the coyotes had been killed out and the jack rabbits increased so tremendously as to be a serious damage to his grass crop, Espy decided that Sam might have been right.

Espy was constantly making improvements on the ranch by building fences, water tanks, corrals, etc. He also planted irrigated fields of Alfalfa.

The original channel of the creek which came out of ZH Canyon ran dangerously close to the ranch house. During the rainy season, when the canyon came down on big rises, it was a constant threat to the house.

In our early years there, Espy expended much hard labor with mules and fresnos [20] building dykes to turn the channel away from the house. In later years, he hired heavy dirt moving machinery to build an entirely new channel for the creek.

---

20 A "fresno" is a horse or tractor drawn blade or scraper designed to grade roads or ditches.

Another improvement in 1929 was his purchase of our first closed car – a secondhand Ford Sedan, which was a vast improvement in comfort over the old open Model T.

+

The lean years came on. Depression is a normal condition in the cattle business, and, when it is compounded by drought, many ranchmen go broke.

Espy was constantly hunting ways to augment our small income from the ranch and to help meet the heavy interest on his debts. In March 1927, he and his Uncle Joe Espy leased the Foley Ranch which joined us on the East for a three-year period. My recollection is that Mr. Joe provided the stock and Espy looked after them, but the arrangement was unsatisfactory and was soon dropped.

Later, Mr. Ed Robbins, a cattle feeder from Belvedere, Kansas, leased the Foley and bought cattle from us. It was he who sent Espy a setting of fine turkey eggs, from which he raised some big turkeys, including a 40-pound Tom. In 1928, Espy was selling calves to an old friend, W.B. ("Mr. Bertie") Mitchell of Marfa for 11 cents a pound.

In 1929 drought forced Espy to move part of his cattle up to his Uncle Judge's ranch at Hot Wells. He leased country from Judge for more than a year until the increasingly severe drought at Hot Wells forced Judge to end the lease.

I have found a letter from J.C. Farmer & Sons, commission men in Ft. Worth, written in 1929, which records the sale of some cows Espy had shipped them for 2 cents a pound! Some calves in the same load brought $3.50 apiece.

About this time Espy was writing to a farmer in Kansas, of whom Mr. Robbins had told him, about selling him some jack rabbits. That was one crop we always had a surplus of!

Espy loved to tell in later life how his family early acquired a taste of brains, tongue, sweetbread, liver and heart, because those were the only parts of the beef we had to eat during those hard times. He often butchered cattle and sold them to markets in neighboring towns and we did eat those interior parts for which there was no sale, but we ate other parts of beef too. Even in the hardest years we ate regularly and well. Although we were already tightening our belts, the full effects of the Great Depression did not reach the ranch industry for a year or more.

Two unexpected windfalls helped us in those hard years. In 1930, Espy was appointed to take the Census of Jeff Davis Co. He devoted three weeks to this job, visiting every home in the county and was paid $600 for it.

We used some of this money to finance our first trip to El Paso. We took the children and spent two days at the old Casa Grande tourist court, enjoying the sights of the city. I still remember the luxuriant red roses everywhere in the valley, and how my desert-starved eyes feasted on the beautifully green cottonwood trees lining the road.

The second windfall was the coming of the "dudes". They came to the ranch in 1929 to talk to Espy about leasing the Holland camp for the purpose of establishing a dude ranch. The man in the deal was George S. Hulings, a self-styled black sheep of a fine old Pennsylvania family.

Like many another black sheep, he was a thoroughly charming and convincing fellow, then in his late fifties. He was well educated and had traveled widely, but had been a lifelong failure financially. His companion was Mrs. E.H. Dodd, wife of the President of Dodd, Meade Publishing Co., already fiftyish and a victim of severe chronic asthma, but still one of most attractive and intelligent women I ever met. Their relationship was to puzzle and worry "Puritanical" Espy all during our acquaintance with them – and forever after!

They were from the same social background and friends of long standing. She was an exile to the West because of her health, but her relations with her husband and grown children were amicable. I am quite convinced that she financed the disastrous venture from the beginning to end.

George Hulings was a dreamer whose life had been spent in the pursuit of get-rich-quick schemes. A younger and far more successful brother, Norman Hulings, was then manager of the Terlingua Mine. Mr. Hulings had known of Camp Holland and had visited it before we bought the ranch. Now he had the dream of turning the abandoned army camp into a fine dude ranch like those he knew in Arizona. He offered to pay Espy $100 a month rent, and Espy accepted thankfully – regardless of his reservations about the couple's morals.

They moved in soon after, accompanied by a cowboy named White, who was cook, dude wrangler and general factotum with other part-time helpers.

Brochure for the Rim Rock Guest Ranch

Mr. Hulings had an attractive brochure advertising *The Rim Rock Ranch* printed and widely distributed among his large circle of acquaintances in the North. They spent much time and considerable money converting the old mess hall into an attractive living and dining room with Western décor. They built a fireplace against the east wall, made a ceiling of Ocotillo stalks from the river and used wagon wheels wired for electricity for light fixtures. The rooms were mainly furnished in crude handmade furniture made by White and painted a bright blue. We later bought many of these furnishings for the proverbial song and used them at the ranch for years.

The venture was doomed to failure because of the timing, for after the market crash in New York, the class of people they had hoped to attract simply quit spending money – at dude ranches or elsewhere. They had few paying guests, but many visitors, including charming Norman Hulings and family.

One of the paying guests was a young man from New York City named Brown, who was completely enamored of the West of his romantic imagination. His fine car contained a regular arsenal of expensive guns, but, to the secret amusement of Mrs. Dodd and scorn of Espy, on reaching Texas, he had bought a pair of secondhand boots.

Espy's fine handmade boots (for he never, even in the leanest years, wore any boots except those custom made for him by G.K. Lange, the famous German boot maker of Alpine) were greatly admired by young Brown. In fact, Espy was the object of his unbounded admiration as he represented his ideas of a cowpuncher.

Espy did not reciprocate. He had had a lifelong scorn of any kind of pretender and of a "tender foot," and he liked nothing better than to deflate one. He took a keen delight in drawing out this dumb boy to enlarge on his ideas of the West, and to tell of his membership in a select New York Club, called "The Ranger Riders of the West". Espy liked to keep him talking on this theme, to the vast secret amusement of Mrs. Dodd and Mr. Hulings, and Brown never caught on to the fact that he was being cruelly ribbed.

I have often told the story, which illustrates Espy's wide acquaintance and friendliness, of a trip Brown persuaded him to make down to the river and across into Mexico. In Marfa where they attended to the necessary legal formalities, Espy naturally knew everyone they met, and, when they got to Presidio, he knew both Mexican and American officials and most of the people on the streets. He even happened to know people in the bar in Ojinaga where they ate lunch.

Late that afternoon, after their return across the bridge, they drove miles down the river among the cotton fields and got lost. A lone man was hoeing cotton in a field near the road. When they stopped to ask direction of him, he greeted them, "Well, hello, Espy, what are you doing down here?" Brown turned to Espy in amazement and asked, "My God, do you know everybody in Texas?"

The dudes stuck it out for twenty-two months. During that time, we lived, thankfully, on the $100 monthly rent they paid us. In addition I made $100 selling them milk, eggs and butter – a sum which I later used for furnishings for the house in Ft. Davis. When they left, they sold everything they could, though some of their equipment was repossessed by the companies they had bought it from.

We bought their Delco plant, as the one we had bought from Mr. Finley had worn out, and some of the furniture, rugs, blankets, etc., all of which we used for many years at the ranch. Espy released Mr. Hulings from the five-year lease they had made, and they parted on friendly terms. It was an interesting experience.

Meanwhile the full force of the Great Depression had finally reached West Texas. Several years of severe drought added to the troubles of the ranch business and ranchmen were "going broke" almost as fast as merchants and banks. But the harder the times were, the greater Espy's determination not to lose the land he had so recently acquired. Besides he had had a lifetime of experiences with depression and drought and it was not as shocking a phenomenon to him as to people in more prosperous parts of the country. So we lived a little harder, and worked longer and got by on less, but we hung on to the ranch.

In 1926 I found the first record of Espy selling calves to W.B. Mitchell and Sons, but I believe he had been doing so long before that, for he had known the Senior Mitchell brothers – "Mr. Tom," "Mr. Arthur," and "Mr. Bertie," and their cousin, "Mr. Crawford" all his adult life. Several of them had at times been in partnership with Joe Espy. They were famous cattlemen, and men of intelligence, character and integrity.

Espy was fond of all of them, but his especial admiration was for "Mr. Bertie" Mitchell who had a vision of the potential greatness of the cattle business in the Big Bend Country, and the ability to carry out his dream. He was the founder of the Highland Hereford Association in 1919 and its first president. He did more to organize and promote the cattle industry in West Texas than any other individual. He was a successful ranchman, but his primary concern was the development of this country. He was a master at promotion. He made innumerable trips into the Corn Belt to sell Highland Cattle, he promoted livestock fairs in Marfa, and entertained hundreds of prospective buyers, with the result that he made the name of Highland Hereford a famous one throughout the whole ranch industry. [21]

Mr. Bertie had always liked Espy and made him a sort of a protege, generously sharing his vision and wide knowledge with the younger man. There is no estimating the broadening effect on Espy's development of Mr. Bertie, nor of the enrichment of his life through the friendship of these three Mitchell brothers. Some of the happiest experiences of his life, especially the Presidency of the Highland Hereford Association and the Swift tour in 1940 grew out of this friendship.

Another person who had a civilizing influence on Espy was my grandmother Foster, who visited us often those early years. Whenever Mother had endured the West as long as she could, or when she was called back to Marlin by illness or death in the family, "Mama" Foster would come out "to help Daughter."

21 The Highland Hereford is a breed of Hereford cattle selectively bred for the Davis Mountains and Big Bend region.

For whatever Mama did was helpful. She adored babies, especially mine, and she was the world's best nurse. She had a large store of stories, songs and games with which she engaged in "training them up in the way they should come". She was a famous cook and an expert seamstress. She taught me cooking by example and precept, but, even with her patience and determination, she was never able to teach me to sew.

She also taught Espy many things, though generally by indirect methods. He admired the strength and depth of her character and came to love her, for everybody loved "Mama". She lived by a high and rigid code, and she expected her descendants to conform to her standards. She and Espy often had disagreements – I recall one over his repairing a screen on Sunday! – but they usually ended in Espy doing as Mama wished, and they only served to increase his respect and affection for her.

He had loved and admired his grandmother Miller, and I think some of his feelings for her carried over into his relationship with my grandmother. Her visits continued after we moved to Ft. Davis, though she grew frailer each time. Just before her death in 1934, Espy drove the children and me to Marlin for one last visit with "Mama".

The children were growing and thriving, though Clay was still small and frail. He suffered constantly from colds and coughs, so in December 1931, we took him to Marlin for a tonsil and adenoid operation. He was only 5, but the doctors felt that the operation was necessary, and it did result in a real improvement in his general health. From then on, he began to grow sturdier.

+

Those early years on the ranch were busy and strenuous ones. There was much to be done in establishing a ranch and a home, and there was never time or money enough to do it all. Espy was continually "improving" – building fences, tanks, dumps to turn water, repairing pipelines and windmills building sheds, salt houses, corrals, and water troughs. There was always some new and vital improvement on the ranch itself to absorb his time and money. He was working desperately hard to meet the interest on the heavy debt.

The fear of losing the ranch hung over him always. He had seen this happen often to ranchmen, and sometimes thru no fault of their own.

Success in the ranch business had never been determined by how expert or industrious a cattleman, was, but depended on outside factors over which he had no control – the weather and the livestock market. We were beset by frequent drought years and record low prices in those early years, and Espy was constantly harassed by financial worries.

How our money should be spent was another continual source of friction between Espy and me. This was a fundamental difference in point of view. Espy had been thoroughly indoctrinated by his mother and his Uncle Joe during his impressionable youth with the ideas that nothing beyond the barest necessities for existence should be spent by a family, and that any profit should either be put back into the ranch or saved.

Mrs. Miller was fond of preaching to me on the virtue of saving – a virtue I considered I had always practiced. None of my family had been wealthy. The only easy times I had ever known had been in early childhood during my father's lifetime, but I had lost him at 14, and Mother and I had lived with strict economy during my High School and College days, until I became the family wage earner upon my graduation from the University of Texas at 20. [22]

I had been partly reared by two grandmothers who had vivid recollections of the desperate poverty of post-Civil War days in Texas, and to whom thrift was as natural as a virtue as industry. But this "genteel" poverty which was still pretty general in the South, even in my youth was nothing like the harsh and grinding poverty the pioneers of this Western country endured.

Espy grew up in this tradition, as did most other people of his day and locality. "A hard school," made harder by the selfishness and stinginess of his mother and his Uncle Joe. These traits were strictly personal ones, and were not characteristic of the West, for many pioneers are neither selfish nor stingy. In fact, an open-handed hospitality to all who came to your door, rude and plain though it might be, was the usual pioneer trait.

Mr. Miller was a completely unselfish man whose first concern always was to provide for his family. He did everything he could to

22 Daughter's father Albert Heard Foster was a dentist and he contracted TB (tuberculosis) from one of his patients. He suffered a long illness, and was sent to a sanatorium, or "tent city" in San Angelo, Texas, because at the time they believed the drier air in places like New Mexico and West Texas would help cure TB. Albert H. Foster died February 12, 1916, when Daughter was 14 years old.

make their lot easier and more comfortable, and to provide for the education of his children. He even helped the children of his brother Bud to get an education – over his wife's opposition, naturally.

He had done what he could to shield his children from the hardships of life in a new country, but he could not shield them from Mrs. Miller's disposition. Like her mother, "Mammy" Espy and her brother Joe, who worshiped money, she rated the acquisition of wealth as the chief aim of life. Joe Espy's growing fortune was a source of enormous pride to Mrs. Miller, regardless of the completely unscrupulous methods used to amass that wealth.

"Aunt Tine" (wife of Uncle Bud Miller) has often told me how angry she used to get at her when they all lived in Valentine, because Lena was always bragging on Joe Espy, and always running Walter down!

Mrs. Miller never appreciated Mr. Miller's many virtues, as a husband and as a man, until he died. Yet he left a legacy of honesty, integrity, industriousness and interest in public service that any man might envy, and he was universally respected and admired in his own community. Nor did "Judge" Espy, the youngest of the tribe, share this trait of inordinate love of money.

Mr. Beau McCutchen told me that Judge was exactly like his father Henry Clay Espy, in appearance and character. His father died when Judge was only six, so his character must have been as much an inheritance as his physical traits, just as his brother, Joe Espy's character and physical appearance were inherited from his mother's family, the Marleys.

I never knew two brothers more different than Judge and Joe Espy. Judge made a considerable financial success during his lifetime, but he made it honestly, by hard labor and good judgement, and without defrauding anybody. Joe Espy would cheat – and did – his own sister and his own sons. Judge loved people and had more friends than any man I ever knew. If Joe Espy ever had a friend, nobody ever heard of it!

The older I grow the more convinced I become of the influence of inheritance on our characters. Like all of us, Espy inherited both good and bad qualities. Physically, he was the "black Marley" type, and unfortunately, he inherited some of their less admirable traits of character also.

I was never able to decide just how many of these undesirable traits, against which I was constantly fighting, were actually inheritance and how many were the result of the influence of his mother and Uncle Joe during his formative years. My son would say that we develop in the way we do because of the particular genes we inherit from various ancestors.

At any rate, Mrs. Miller and Mr. Joe were the dominant influences in Espy's youth, and not his father. But Mr. Miller was the most influential factor in Keesey's and Audrey's lives, for they were more like him. Both of them were pure Millers.

Espy admired his father, and loved him more deeply than he ever loved anyone else in his life, I think, but he was not like him. The one major inheritance he got was his aptitude with tools. All the Millers were expert with their hands, and clever at mechanics and building, but Espy used to say that none of the Espys could drive a nail in straight!

In these early years of our marriage, Espy was still much influenced by the training and indoctrination he had received during his years of slavery under Mr. Joe. Even though he had finally rebelled against Mr. Joe's dictatorial ways, and had broken with him, he was still unconsciously patterning his life on Mr. Joe's, and his greatest ambition was to get rich.

But he lacked Mr. Joe's ruthlessness, and this ambition was mitigated by the probity his father had taught him. As he matured, he gradually came to realize that his father's life was not only more admirable, but also more desirable than his Uncle Joe's. But the damage Mrs. Miller and Mr. Joe had done to his character was done in his early years, and it was many years before he was to grow out of it. In fact, the break with Mr. Joe was not actually complete until Mr. Joe caused Keesey's defeat in a race for county commissioner many years later.

Other broadening influences were at work on Espy, his many friendships with guests at the hotel, his widening circle of friends, especially his Uncle Judge, "Mr. Bertie," and Judge J.C. Fuller, his growing children, his enlarging vision as he moved in constantly widening circles – and my constant opposition to his placing financial values before human ones, all contributed to a gradual change in many of his ideas and prejudices. But the changes were slow and painful to both of us.

Next to the continual trouble with both our mothers, disagreements over money were the next most divisive force in our marriage. Espy's natural largeness and generosity of nature were constantly at war with the penuriousness which had been ingrained into him as a youth. He loved to make extravagant gifts to those he loved.

Over the years, he made me many beautiful gifts, and he enjoyed giving them as much as I did receiving them. But the monthly bills for groceries, drugs, clothes and other expenses necessary to a growing family nearly drove him crazy.

Yet, even in those hard times, he was making lavish gifts – boxes of the choicest Ft. Davis apples to Uncle Zenas Bartlett and Milton Davison, and always a quarter of beef to the Christmas family reunion in Marlin. I have found a letter from Mr. Robert Calder, a dear friend from Galveston, in 1933, thanking him for a quarter of beef.

Another trait that mitigated his concern over expenses was his hospitality. He loved and enjoyed people. One of his most conspicuous traits was that he never liked to be alone – the natural result, I suspect, of having been too much alone in his bachelor days. He always wanted somebody "helping" him at any job he was doing – actually it was their company he wanted.

The children were always around him when he was working around the place, and as soon as he had taught them to ride, he insisted on their accompanying him on horseback whenever possible. I've often known of him picking up a stray Mexican child for company, rather than be alone. He wanted me "Helping" him whenever he went to the barn, the shop or the garden or where ever he was at work. I was generally too busy with my own numerous tasks to accompany him, but he never ceased trying to get me to go with him.

From our very earliest days at the ranch we had a constant and never ending stream of company. We were at the end of the road, so guests had to be fed, and often "bedded down" for the night. Espy took a keen pleasure in showing off the ranch and the improvements he was constantly making.

He was proud of his attractive home and of his family, and he took great pride in being what "Bama" Conoly [23] called "a good provider". Fresh beef, chickens and eggs, milk, butter, abundant

23 Daughter's grandmother, Mary Jane Keesee, born July 11, 1849 in Arkansas and died June 15, 1930 in Marlin, Texas.

vegetables and fruits in season, and large stores of home canned fruits, preserves, jellies, etc., helped supply the good meals he so thoroughly enjoyed and enjoyed sharing with guests.

The Holland Ranch had one asset that many West Texas ranches lacked – an abundant water supply. The spring in ZH Canyon provided an ample supply of water for the cattle, house and yard, and was, when we bought the ranch, the only source of water except the Buford windmill in the flat.

Even in the worst droughts, this spring never did run completely dry, tho it often got low enough in a dry spring that we rationed water carefully in house and garden. And many times, due to burst pipes or other troubles, we were temporarily without water, and sometimes had to haul water for use at the house by the barrel full from the Buford windmill.

The regular supervision of this complicated water supply, miles of pipe line, rock and dirt tanks and water troughs was one of Espy's chief tasks, for only by constant vigilance on his part were all of them kept functioning. Like all cowpunchers of his day, he was expert at windmill and well repair. Windmill repairs was one of the most hazardous of a cowpuncher's tasks and many accidents resulted from it. Espy was lucky in that he never had a serious accident with a windmill, though he had many narrow escapes.

I was gradually losing most of my fears of this strange new country, but one fear I never conquered was fear of rattlesnakes. Neither did Espy. Rattlesnakes were the only thing I know of that he was actually afraid of, but that fear only made him more determined to kill every one he encountered. I have watched, always with horror, many of his battles with them – using sticks, rocks, tire chains, pieces of pipe – anything that came to hand to kill them. I recall one especially horrifying episode when he tried to pin one down with a dagger stalk, and the stalk broke under him! But even that one did not escape.

Rattlesnakes were not as common on the ranch, due I suppose to the extermination of their chief food supply, the prairie dog, as they had been in Espy's youth. Then, he often said, it was not uncommon to kill 40 or 50 on a morning's cattle drive. But we had enough to keep us eternally vigilant. Over the years, we lost many horses, cows and dogs, even cats, to rattlesnake bites, but the thing I lived in constant dread of – one of the children being bitten by a rattlesnake – never happened.

We had our share of accidents. At least three times after our marriage – no telling how many times before! – Espy narrowly escaped death by being thrown by horses. Twice he suffered broken ribs from these falls, and was laid up in bed for days with excruciating pain.

Once his horse stepped in a prairie dog hole and fell with Espy. The horse then panicked and started to run, and only the fact that his foot, which had hung in one stirrup, slipped out of his boot and thus freed him, saved him from being dragged to death.

His last accident with a horse occurred shortly before World War II, when, as he always said, his horse reared up with him and "sat down on him" injuring his right knee so seriously as to cripple him for months and eventually necessitating major surgery on the knee.

All this, and many minor accidents and escapes, in spite of the fact that Espy was an expert horseman. They were just the normal occupational hazards of a cowpuncher, and almost every cowhand of his generation whose life, like Espy's had largely been spent in the saddle, had had his share of accidents.

I always thought that Espy was the most beautiful rider I ever saw. He and his horse seemed to be one piece. He loved good horses and his own mounts were always chosen with great care. To begin with, because of his weight, they had to be unusually big horses, and they had to have "cowsense" and "bottom" for the long rides and arduous work with cattle.

Beyond this he demanded that they satisfy his standards of beauty in a horse, and they were invariably handsome animals. He also demanded spirit in them, and his favorite horses, Eagle, Chico, Paprika, Joe Lewis, Ramon and many others were usually so spirited that nobody else could ride them.

When he worked for Mr. Joe, part of his job had been breaking horses, but he did not like the chore. More, I think, because he disliked the cruelty to horses it involved than from fear, and he always preferred to buy horses that were already broken, or to hire someone to do that job.

Although Espy had a genuine love for horses, as he did for all animals, he had no silly sentiment about them. They were tools of his trade, to be used wisely and to be taken care of properly. But he also had an unusual amount of understanding and sympathy for animals, perhaps because his life had largely been spent in close association with them.

He was patient and solicitous in his treatment of both horses and cattle, and would never permit any abuse of or cruelty to them. Nothing angered him more than to see a man abuse a horse. I remember his fury at a famous rodeo performer, Bob Crosly whom we once saw in an Alpine rodeo because the man was so cruel to his horses.

Espy never relaxed his vigilant concern over his stock, and rode the ranch constantly in close supervision of his herd, sometimes alone, sometimes accompanied by Mexicans or the children. He attended the cows with especial solicitude during the time of calving and with such great concern for their welfare and suffering that I have accused him of having more sympathy for cows than for women!

As pickups gradually began to supplant horses on the work of the ranches, Espy used his pickup in place of a horse, and, I used to think, in much the same way! He expected a pickup to go anywhere a horse could go and his habit of driving over the open range terrified and battered his passengers.

Many is the wild chase after a stray coyote that I have made with him in the pickup – his driving so fast and furious and rough that I expected the children and me to be thrown out momentarily! And many the bumpy ride I have had with him on his tours of inspection of isolated tanks, stray bands of cattle, or broken-down fences or phone lines. These were the occupational hazards of a ranch wife, and one I never really learned to enjoy.

Also, it was the duty of the wife to open gates. They were plentiful in early years and were generally rude wire gaps, so heavy and so tightly hung that it was often beyond my strength to open one. I **HATED** opening gates, as I hated doing anything mechanical, and also because I felt it was not a suitable task for a woman.

Consequently, Espy took a fiendish delight in making me try to open every one, as a part of his program of training me to be a proper ranchwoman. So he would always make me try to open any gate, and would watch my futile and increasingly furious struggles with the obstinate gate with amusement, even though he knew all the time that he would eventually have to get out and open - and also shut! – the gate.

Judging by the frequency with which this situation appears in Ace Reid's [24] cowboy cartoons, I am sure that many ranch wives have shared this particular "bête noir" with me.

Even though horses became less important in ranch work with the increasing use of pickups, they were never, at least for us, completely superseded. Espy always kept an adequate remuda and was constantly replacing old horses with new.

His own taste in horses altered with age too, and his last horse, faithful old Streak, though big and powerful and full of cowsense, was so gentle that he allowed Espy to carry a couple of grandchildren, fore and aft, on him. After Espy died, Clay's wife, Jody took Streak for her horse, though she was so small she needed help to mount him, and like Espy she worked cattle on him with a baby in the saddle in front of her.

Though Espy had no fear of horses, he had plenty of respect for them, and he exercised great care about who rode them. He was especially careful about which horses were ridden by guests or children, for most ranch horses are not suited to "tenderfeet". He began teaching his own children to ride almost before they could walk.

Great was my suffering when he insisted on carrying one of my precious babies in the saddle in front of him on one of his high-spirited horses! But Espy knew his horses better than I did and he was supremely confident of his ability to control them. Also, he was determined to train his children to be good cowpunchers and that training, in his opinion, could not be begun too young.

As soon as Clay was born, he began searching for suitable children's horses; he was still searching for horses suitable for his grandchildren when he died. But after his first disastrous attempts to teach me to ride in the early months of our marriage, he never tried to find a horse for me, and much as he hated to admit it, he was forced into the realization that I couldn't ride a horse!

He started Clay riding Chico, when he was still a little fellow with long hair, as a Kodak picture of them shows, at first around the yard, later, with a leading string, outside in the flats. Chico was a pretty palomino from the river who was gentle enough for Clay at first, but eventually became too much horse for a child to ride.

24 Ace Reid was a syndicated "cowboy cartoonist." His "Cowpoke" cartoons were especially appreciated by those trying to make a living on the land.

Espy searched for a long time for suitable ponies for Clay and Betty, and finally found a pair of half-starved Mexican ponies from the river who proved to be perfect. Clay's was a gray pony called "Tapon" and Betty's was a bay named "Tajon".

Tapon lasted during Clay's and Betty's childhood and served them well, but "Tajonie" lived to extreme old age, and was the most beloved horse we ever owned. Not only did all our children, and all their relatives and friends learned to ride on the patient animal, but he even lasted thru another generation, and all of the grandchildren, except Elizabeth and Dave, also learned to ride on him. He was a perfect children's horse.

Besides those due to horses, there were plenty of other accidents on the ranch. Our nephew, "K.K." Miller, was to express it succinctly many years later when he remarked that "we lived in a state of crisis on the ranch". This was literally true, and we had, it sometimes seemed, more than our share of accidents and of natural catastrophes – floods, fires, lightning, and even a major earthquake. One of the first accidents happened when Clay was about two. He was running around the back yard with a little stick in his mouth when he tripped and fell and rammed a splinter from the stick down his throat. We called Dr. Vick and he came immediately, but he was so nervous and upset that he could not pull the splinter out. So he finally held the child while Espy took a small pair of pliers and expertly extracted every particle of the splinter from Clay's throat.

The following year when Betty was about 18 months old, she fell out of the low branches of a peach tree, late in the afternoon, while Espy and I were busily engaged in setting out tomato plants. She only fell a couple of feet, but, unluckily, an old iron plow was lying under the tree, and its exposed edge cut a horrible gash in her mouth and cheek. We drove to Marfa in record time. There was then stationed at Fort D.A. Russell a fine surgeon – Major Clark. We owe him eternal gratitude. He gave Betty tetanus shots, and took forty stitches in her cheek and mouth, and did the job so skillfully that no scar was left, and, in years to come, neither Betty nor I could remember which side of her face was cut.

One of the many helpful purchases Mr. Miller made for us was second-hand electric wood saw. [25] This tool made the perpetual chore of supplying firewood for the kitchen stove and living room fireplace much easier and quicker, but it was also extremely dangerous. One day while sawing wood, Espy's hand slipped, and, in a second the whole top of his right hand was cut to ribbons. We put a tourniquet on his arm, and wrapped the bloody hand in towels and left at once for Ft. Davis. Espy insisted on driving with his left hand, because he could drive faster than I could. We went straight to the office of Dr. C.E. Eaton. He worked long and carefully at the delicate task of sewing the torn muscles and nerves together, and did such an expert job that Espy eventually regained complete use of the damaged hand. I always had more respect for Dr. Eaton's professional skill after this. He had Espy exercise the hand constantly while it was healing, by constantly handling a small rubber ball and by milking.

There were scary times at the ranch sometimes when ZH Canyon would come down on a big rise, and the raging creek would come dangerously close to the house. Espy was constantly having dumps made to turn it away from the house, and eventually hired a crew with heavy dirt moving machinery to dig an entire new channel for the overflow.

In summer during heavy rains we were often marooned at the ranch for days on end. The roads were bad in good weather and impassable in wet. Also, the Wild Horse Draw would frequently come down on a big rise, and cut us off completely from Valentine. More than once, rises carried off the frail bridge which Espy and his men would have to replace.

The telephone was a constant source of irritation, as it worked only intermittently. Espy spent much time "riding" the line, looking for broken wires. Lightning would sometimes strike the line, or cattle would rub down posts, or some trouble would develop in the antiquated switchboard. The old Delco plant also had to be nursed along carefully and had to be replaced more than once before the arrival of REA in the 1950s. [26]

Refrigeration was another problem. At first the old cement water trough in the milk house furnished the only refrigeration we had. Finally,

25 "The saw was powered by a belt to the Farmall tractor." Clay Espy Miller, Jr.
26 REA, The Rural Electrification Administration a New Deal agency created in 1933 to provide loans and technical support to electrify rural areas primarily through Co-operatives.

Espy bought a second-hand (we rarely bought anything new!) Kerosene refrigerator, called a Superflex. This was a vast improvement over the milk trough, but it was temperamental and the Kerosene fire which ran it had to be fed and lighted every twenty-four hours. We depended on this Superflex, however, until the advent of butane gas into the country.

✣

Almost our only social life during the first years at the ranch was a constant succession of guests. We went little ourselves – to Ft. Davis occasionally to visit Espy's family and the Hunter Clarks, to Marfa sometimes to buy groceries and clothes and shoes for the children at the old Murphy-Walker store, to Alpine rarely to see a doctor or to spend a day with our friends, Douglas and Lucy McMurry. But we had many guests at the ranch, especially in summer.

We had visits from many members of Espy's family and mine. The Arthur Threadgills, Willett Fosters and Zenas Bartletts all visited us at the ranch. Judge and Buelah Espy, who lived on their ranch near Hot Wells, were frequent visitors.

Our earliest friends, the Van Neils, had sold their ranch to the Kimballs of Alpine and had moved to the El Paso Valley. A kindly old couple named Carr, who worked for the Kimballs, lived in their old house. Later a young cowhand named Joe Wilson lived there. Ed Hunter, who ran the Conring house South of us, was a longtime friend of Espy's. We saw him frequently as he always helped out at round up time and with other work.

Our closest friends in those years were Ben and Lilla Morris, who had moved to Valentine from deep East Texas, and had bought the grocery store from George Newton, about the time we moved to the ranch. They felt like exiles, as I did, and a close friendship grew up between us. They built a pretty little home in Valentine which Lilla furnished charmingly with antiques bought from the antebellum McWhorter home in Douglasville.

Lilla was an old-fashioned Southern lady, of unusual charm and beauty, and possessed of a keen mind and lively wit. Like many Southern women of the old school, she was a superb cook, but she had the unheard-of luxury (for Valentine) of a Negro cook. This was Jerome, descended of McWhorter slaves and a former chef on the Southern

Pacific Railroad, who worked for her intermittently. Some of the best meals I have ever eaten were the products of Lilla's and Jerome's skills.

There was one memorable meal prepared by Jerome however, that was not enjoyed by hosts or guests. Espy and the children and I were visiting with the Morris' in front of their store one afternoon, following a trip to Marfa, where Espy had bought, among other things, some sacks of poisoned grain to use on a prairie dog colony in the flat. These paper sacks were on the floor of the back seat, along with our groceries and the children.

Presently we discovered, to our horror that Betty was eating some of the poisoned grain. We frantically thought of antidotes and someone suggested egg white. Lilla hastily brought a cup of egg whites from the store and began pouring it down Betty, when Clay remarked calmly, "You'd better give me some, 'cause I ate it too!" We were afraid to go to the ranch and get further away from help, so Lilla insisted on our going up to her house for supper, where we could watch for developments.

This we did, but nobody enjoyed that meal, or even knew what they were eating. We had rigors when either child wanted a drink, because we remembered that poisoned animals always craved water. At bed time when the children still seemed all right, we went home. They did not suffer any ill results from the frightening experience. Later the man who mixed the poisoned grain told Espy that he was in the habit of tasting it to see if he had gotten it strong enough!

We had many acquaintances and some close friends among the summer guests at the hotel. Among the latter were Orland Sims of Paint Rock and Mr. and Mrs. Robert J. Calder of Galveston. These and many others visited us at the ranch. I have often regretted that I did not keep a guest book back in those days.

There were interesting contacts other than social. The summer after we moved to the ranch, a group of about two dozen entomologists from the University of Kansas asked for and got permission to set up a camp and collect specimens in our flat. They stayed several weeks and said that the location was a veritable paradise for entomologists. Among them was a young woman, a librarian, who later married our neighbor from "Under the Rim," Evans Means. [27]

27 "Under the Rim" is the area below the Sierra Vieja cliffs to the Rio Grande.

In 1932, Espy, still searching for chances to augment our income, entered into partnership with a neighbor, Den Knight, whose ranch was about twenty miles east of us. They bought about 1,300 sheep and 70 cattle which were to be pastured on the Knight ranch. The sheep feature of this enterprise proved to be disastrous financially, as the price of lambs and wool dropped, and both Espy and Den took considerable loss. In spite of the business failure though, they remained friends.

It was sometime during this ill-fated adventure in sheep that some scientists from the Smithsonian Institute came to the Knight ranch and began an investigation of an old Indian cave there. Espy's wide range of curiosity embraced every field of knowledge he encountered, no matter how far removed from his normal pursuits.

So he spent considerable time watching the archaeologists at work, and (I'm quite sure) pumping them for information about what they were doing. He was fascinated by the care with which they removed and sifted the dirt from the cave, and by the items they found in it; tiny ears of corn, turkey bones and the skeleton of a child wrapped in a woven basket. They told him that they believed this civilization was probably the same as that of the earliest basket makers at Mesa Verde. From this time on Espy had a keen interest in Indian Archeology, an interest I had long had, and one that was passed on to our children.

We had experiences over the years with many varieties of violence of nature, the constant winds and wild Spring dust storms, an occasional small tornado, drought, floods, blizzards and deluges, but on August 17, 1931, we had a new experience – a major earthquake. [28]

The Valley between the Sierra Vieja range and the Davis Mountains was the bottom of an inland sea in prehistoric times. We had heard rumors in Valentine of small earthquakes in times past. Early in the morning of that day, we were aroused from sleep by preliminary tremors of what was unmistakably an earthquake.

My mother, who slept in the big north room, felt it first. Judge and Beulah Espy were in the little back room, and Espy and I on the

28 Early in the morning of August 16, 1931 Valentine and the surrounding area was hit by an earthquake. It was determined to be an 8.0 on the Richter Scale, and it did serious damage, especially to adobe structures.

sleeping porch, with Clay and Betty in their beds on each side of ours. We had each grabbed a child and started for the front door of the sleeping porch when the heavy shock began.

An earthquake is an indescribable sensation, like nothing else in the world. I shall never forget the horror of feeling our way down the long front porch, with the thick adobe wall beside us trembling like a leaf in the wind and the floor buckling beneath our feet. It seemed certain that the walls would collapse on us and our babies before we could reach the door, but the shock subsided just as we did.

Mother had run out of the front door ahead of us, and Judge and Buelah had run out of the door on the back porch. Just seconds after Buelah had rushed out, the entire cement top of one big chimney crashed down on the spot she had just passed. We huddled in the yard in our nightclothes wondering if this was the end for us, while almost incessant small tremors added to our terror.

There was an unearthly light over everything, and we could see clouds of dust or smoke boiling out of the canyons, and could hear the roar of falling rocks. A loud rumbling came from inside the earth under our feet.

The poor animals were in panic – chickens squawking, dogs barking, cattle and horses running madly in every direction. We wondered whether we had already had the major shock, or whether it was still ahead of us. The house was a shambles. Both chimney tops had fallen off, the plaster had fallen off the house inside and out, dishes, bottles, pictures had been dashed to the floor, and great cracks in the thick adobe walls had opened above the doors. We dressed ourselves in the yard and realized that we were hungry.

I followed Espy into the kitchen where he started a fire in the wood stove, for the flue seemed undamaged, and amid the wreckage, began to assemble breakfast for us. We were still badly frightened and whenever a slight tremor occurred, we would dash out into the yard again. But we finally got food ready and the table on the back porch sufficiently cleared of debris to eat off of. Nobody had much appetite, though Buelah always afterwards recalled the delicious cantaloupes we had.

While we were eating, a car came tearing up to the back gate. It was our good neighbor, Ed Hunter, who had come over to see how we had survived the shock. When he saw we were safe, he went into hysterics, his thin body alternately racked with uncontrollable tears and laughter. We discussed what to do next. It was obviously impossible to stay in the wrecked house. The phone was out, of course, and, except for Ed's report, we had no idea of the extent of the damage. But we all felt that the only thing possible was to go to Ft. Davis. So we loaded clothes and children into the car and fled to Ft. Davis. Judge and Buelah went in the opposite direction to Hot Wells.

The center of the shock, we later learned, had been an area of some twenty miles around Valentine, which included the ranch. Valentine was a village of adobe houses and many of them were in ruins. None had escaped serious damage; many of them were on the ground in ruins. The inhabitants were in a state of panic.

Miraculously, among all the falling walls of adobe buildings, nobody had been killed, though in Terlingua, nearly a hundred miles to the East, a man down in the mines was killed by falling rocks. At Ft. Davis there was little damage, though they had felt the shocks sharply. This was rated as a major earthquake by geologists, the only one in Texas' recorded history – and we were right in the center of it! [29]

We spent three weeks at the hotel in Ft. Davis, though Espy was making daily trips back to the ranch to look after the stock and to ascertain further damage. As the shocks decreased, our terror lessened, and he finally decided that we would have to return to our home, regardless of our fears of more earthquakes.

So we went, followed by Mr. Miller, Mr. Neal Adriance of Galveston and Senator Tom Love [30] of Dallas, both of whom were frequent guests at the hotel and old friends. Espy also took along a couple of Mexican workmen to repair the house. I have a vivid memory of fixing a fried chicken dinner for the crowd amid the shambles of a kitchen!

Espy had borrowed two tents and these were set up in the front yard under the locust trees and our beds moved out into them. We slept there until cold weather in late November drove us indoors. The Mexicans and Espy went to work, moving furniture onto the porch, cleaning out the debris, mending cracks in the adobe walls and

29 Another large earthquake was recorded in Brewster County on April 14, 1995 – the 5.7 Cathedral Mountain Earthquake.
30 State Senator Tom Love of Dallas was a frequent visitor to Fort Davis and actively promoted the region. He was primarily responsible for the legislation that created the Davis Mountains State Park.

replastering them, replacing the heavy cement and brick tops of the chimneys, and repainting.

Finally the house was habitable again, and we reluctantly moved back inside. It was years, however, before I could sleep without fear at the ranch. For over a year after the earthquake, frequent tremors were felt. Some people slept in their cars all winter. A wild rumor circulated through the village that a fortune teller had predicted that exactly a year after the first one, another earthquake would occur which would destroy Valentine. When early in the morning of August 17, 1932, a distinctly perceptible shock was felt, the panic in the village may be imagined!

That last year we spent on the ranch was an uncomfortable one, with the terrifying memory of the earthquake always in our minds. But Espy and I were learning as we grew older; to face the future with more courage. I had to put on a brave front for the sake of the children, and not allow them to see how frightened I really was. How much courage in just putting on a brave front!

✦

Clay was six years old on July 7, 1932, and the question of his education had to be solved. Hard as times were, a governess was out of the question. We never considered moving to Valentine. Ft. Davis had always been home to Espy, and it seemed the natural place for us to go.

With his heavy burden of debt on the ranch, Espy had no money to buy a house in town or even rent one. Just at this time my mother had come into a little legacy from Grandmother Conoly's estate (the last residue of the great Brazos bottom plantation called Hog Island that her grandfather, Henry Lightfoot Bennett, had established in the 1840s). [31]

One of Espy's friends, R.C. Williams, held a mortgage on an old house in Ft. Davis, then occupied by the Otis Grubb family and he was eager to sell the place. Since he knew we needed a place in town to live, he offered to sell this house for $3,500.

After considerable thought, Mother decided to invest Grandma's legacy in this house. We made a trip to Ft. Davis to look at it. From the moment I walked in the front door, I loved the old house, and knew it could be home to us, despite the deplorable state of repair it was in.

31 Henry Littleton Bennett was born December 6, 1808 in Tennessee and died September 20, 1881 in Reagan, Texas.

Mother bought the house and in late August 1932 we moved in and a new phase of our life began.

With the exception of a few secondhand things, we had bought very little furniture since our marriage. We had been able to furnish the ranch house comfortably with mother's old furniture, a few things Espy had inherited from his Miller grandparents, some pieces he or his father had made, and a few things we bought from "the dudes".

Now we were faced with the problem of furnishing a fourteen-room house in Ft. Davis, and of leaving enough at the ranch for Espy to "batch" and for the needs of the family when we returned to the ranch for the summers. I still remember how bare the big old rooms in the Ft. Davis house looked at first with our skimpy furnishings distributed over them.

Espy moved all the furniture, even Mother's piano, from the ranch to town in a trailer pulled by the family car, for he still had no pickup. It was a very rainy fall, and every trip was made over almost impassibly muddy roads. Mother's much traveled old furniture presented a very bedraggled appearance on its final arrival in Ft. Davis.

The move was further complicated by a house guest for my devoted friend of University days, Martha Rivers Allen of Bryan, had come out for a visit, which rather inopportunely, coincided with our move. But Martha Rivers was a rare spirit, blessed with sensitivity, charm and irrepressible gaiety. She took the inconveniences in her stride, and by her helpfulness and constant high spirits, treated the whole move as high adventure and greatly lightened our lagging spirits.

The old house was in a dreadful state of repair. It had been completely made over and greatly enlarged (by the addition of the front hall, two big North rooms and the half story above) by Mr. Bill Jones about 1910 when he moved his family to town to go to school.

The original house, consisting of what is now the guest bedroom, back hall and bath and my south bedroom, had been built in 1883 by a lawyer named F.W. Colby. At some later date the kitchen and little dining room had been added. Many different families had occupied the house over its long life. It looked rather hopeless when we moved in – with a worn-out roof which leaked in dozens of places, paint peeling and plaster falling off the walls, floors worn out and splintery, and the improvised bathroom a hopeless mess.

Mother hired a carpenter to replace the rotted floor in the little front bedroom and to make over the bathroom completely. Espy worked with the carpenter in repairing the plumbing and in mending the worst holes in the roof. Mr. Miller gave us everything he could think of to help with the repair and furnishings.

We began with a Herculean cleaning job. Espy and I Kalsomined all the big rooms, even the ceilings, and spread a small amount of paint where it would do the most good. Mother, who had a real talent for interior decoration, gradually distributed the old furnishings until the house began to look more like a home.

I used the $100 I had made selling butter, milk and eggs to the dudes to buy a few new furnishings from the Montgomery Ward catalog, shades, bed springs, a $14 rug (which I still use!) and other essentials. Mother took the front room as her bedroom, and Espy and the children and I lived in the South bedroom. The big north room at the back of the house became the living room. It was heated by a big old pot-bellied coal stove Uncle Willett sent us from Marlin. Coal could then be bought at the railroad in Marfa and was about as cheap as wood. There was a fireplace in our bedroom, and we put small cheap tin stoves in Mother's room and in the upstairs bedrooms.

We had hardly gotten moved when I acquired a boarder. This was Doris Everett, daughter of our friends and distant neighbors in Valentine, the Noel Everetts, who was then working in the Fort Davis State Bank. This was in the midst of the Great Depression and the prospect of any supplementing of our scanty income was too tempting to be denied. Besides we had the big old empty house and cooking was one of my few accomplishments, so I welcomed this opportunity to help out.

Espy was bitterly opposed from the first, and all thru the period, to my keeping boarders. It hurt his pride cruelly. But we were in such desperate straits financially that he grudgingly consented. So Doris moved into the little front bedroom upstairs and began paying me $25 monthly for board and room. Almost immediately I had four other boarders, Knox and Lou Reid, who were both teaching in the school, another schoolteacher named Cohn, and a highway construction engineer named Short. The Reids occupied the big front bedroom downstairs, Mr. Short had what is now Betty's room and Mr. Cohn, Clay's. There was, of course, only the one bathroom downstairs, Mr. Cohn, who was an abysmally selfish person, made the bathroom congestion worse!

For the next three years, with no breaks except for the summers at the ranch, I had these same boarders. If the early years at the ranch had been hard, these were harder. I worked harder than ever before or since, but I was young and strong and also determined to make a success of the venture.

With Mother's help, I did all the cooking, housecleaning and dishwashing. We had an old Mexican woman who did the washing, in the kitchen, boiling clothes in a big copper boiler on the kitchen stove.

Table linens were a great problem as this was before the day of the universal paper napkin. It helped a little to use napkin rings to keep the ownership of napkins straight. During that time, most of our old linens were worn out, and all of Mother's lovely old gold banded china was broken up. We had a succession of inexperienced Mexican girls to wash dishes, but they were all so incompetent and so slovenly that we finally dispensed altogether with their so-called help, and did the washing, a "perpetual chore" ourselves.

I practiced the most rigid economy and the help of meat, milk, eggs, fruit and vegetables in season which Espy brought from the ranch, I was able to stretch my $100 monthly income to cover the grocery bill for both family and boarders. I still have a letter I wrote to Mama Foster in 1933, which she saved, telling of my agonizing fear that I would lose my boarders when I had to increase the monthly fee to $30! But I didn't. They stayed with me, and Doris and the Reids remained good friends for the rest of our lives.

For Espy, the move to town began his long year of commuting. His early years of "batching" had given him an intense hatred of living alone. No man ever enjoyed the comforts of home and family more than he did. He deeply resented the necessary separation from his wife and children, but it was a problem common to ranch life, and made even more necessary by the extreme financial depression. So he endured it grudgingly and usually got back to Ft. Davis on weekends to spend a few days with his family.

We were both overworked and harassed almost beyond endurance by financial worries and domestic tensions, yet our mutual love, despite all of our disagreements and difficulties, deepened with each passing year.

Mother was perceptive enough to realize this and it only intensified her jealousy and hatred of Espy, both of which she became less and less able to conceal as time went on. His dislike and resentment of her were equally great, but we were held together in an inescapable net of circumstances. It was her home we lived in, yet increasingly, as the money my father left in 1916 diminished, she was dependent on Espy for support.

The problems of trying to keep the peace between these two domineering natures, and of trying to "keep the surface smooth" for the boarders, and of making a normal and happy home for my children, were always my most difficult tasks. Compared to the intense emotional strain under which I lived, constantly torn between my duty to my mother and my love for my husband, the hard realities of poverty and drudgery were trifles.

Dear Uncle Willett once told me that I was in the position of a bone between two dogs. But he and all the other members of my family realized that Mother was the one insoluble problem in our marriage. More and more their sympathy was for Espy, though their pity and love for "poor Lute" never ceased. She realized that she was losing the support of her family, and it only served to infuriate her and to intensify her persecution complex.

Her frequent trips back to Marlin were the only peaceful periods in our lives, but no urging by all the members of her family could persuade her to stay away from "Daughter". She would permit neither advice or criticism in this matter. Her adored nephew, Conoly Bartlett, once attempted to persuade her to leave Ft. Davis and move back to Marlin, and by his well-meant efforts, effectively killed her love for him for the rest of her life.

As she grew older, she became more bitter and overbearing and increasingly parasitic on me. Her morbid jealousy of Espy consumed her, and eventually verged on insanity. If only I had had the wisdom and the courage in those years to agree to Espy's continual pleadings, and to insist that she leave us and go back to Austin or Marlin, how infinitely better and happier life would have been not only for us, but also for poor, tormented mother. My rigid sense of duty to a parent forced me to keep on trying to reconcile two irreconcilable natures and brought only unhappiness to us and tragedy to her.

My relations with Mrs. Miller, on the contrary, improved as those with my own mother worsened. She gradually came to accept me as Espy's wife, and even to take some pride in the amount of work I did.

Besides, Keesey had married Lillian Yarbro in 1929, so I had help in the daughter-in-law field! I made up my mind to treat Mrs. Miller with politeness and courtesy regardless of what she did or said, and to keep out of her way as much as possible. This policy paid off well, and our relations from this time on were quite amicable, though hardly affectionate.

+

Meanwhile Espy's financial difficulties were increasing as the depression deepened and were compounded by one of the most severe droughts we ever experienced. Espy used to say that in the cattle business you could usually manage to weather low prices and depressions, but it was drought that broke you.

His old friend, Al Driffel, who had loaned him money to buy the ranch, was headed for financial ruin as the depression ruined the market for quicksilver. He also had a family of fourteen children and a sick wife. His letters to Espy increasingly became agonized pleas for money, any money that Espy could spare to pay on his loan might help him stave off impending ruin.

As early as 1924, Judge J.C. Fuller, first Secretary of the Marfa National Farm Loan Association, had offered Espy a loan from the Federal Land Bank, but he had not taken the loan then. Judge Fuller remained an interested and close friend to Espy, and like Mr. Bertie Mitchell, took an almost paternal interest in him. Thru his help, Espy obtained a loan of $40,000 from the Land Bank on Oct. 31, 1933. He used this money to repay Al Driffel and small loans from the Fort Davis State Bank.

From that time on, the Federal Land Bank was our only [32] creditor. Their generous long-term loans and low rate of interest lessened one of Espy's heaviest worries. He became convinced of the great value to ranchman of this particular program. Before 1936, he was elected Director of the Marfa Farm Loan Association, a position he held until his death.

Since depression is endemic in the ranch business in West Texas, the blighting effect of the Great Depression did not begin to be felt until a year or more after they had paralyzed the rest of the nation. Cattle prices fell to a new low, and there was no demand for cattle at any price, as few people had money enough to buy meat. Then came the terrible drought years.

32 "Espy borrowed modest amounts through the years for operating expenses from the Fort Davis State Bank."Clay Espy Miller, Jr.

This was the era of the "Dust Bowl", a national disaster, when the plowed fields of Oklahoma, Kansas and a great section of the Midwest simply dried up and blew away. Much of it blew into West Texas. We began having dust storms of a very different kind from the native West Texas variety.

Wind and dust were old enemies here, and wild dust storms were a regular and normal hazard of life. But these dust storms were different. They came oozing slowly in from the North. A thick curtain of red dust that moved slowly over the sky until the sun itself was blotted out, and day became almost as dark as night. The air was as thick as soup with the brick red dust. Even inside houses you could hardly breathe. The dust hung in the atmosphere for hours and days, as one spell followed fast on the heals of the last. People wore masks on their faces and put wet sheets and towels over doors and windows and around children's beds. The thick air choked you and burned your eyes, and caused widespread epidemics of all sorts of respiratory troubles. Babies and old Folks died.

People wondered uneasily what the unnatural atmosphere portended; some speculated that it was the end of the world. It was the end of the world for many people, as the combination of depression and drought destroyed the economic foundation of America. The Great Depression was a traumatic experience. Those of us who lived through it never fully recovered from its effects. It destroyed our faith in the "American Dream".

Never again would we take security for granted. It was the second great shock (the first World War had been the first) for my generation of idealistic humanists, who had actually believed in human perfectibility and who had confidently expected to usher in the Millennium by their own efforts. The final shock, of course, was our unwilling recognition of what our ancestors called Original Sin, forced on us when World War II revealed to us the depths of human depravity.

For ranch men there was no way out. There was no grass anywhere to which their starving cattle could be moved, as virtually all the range land in the U.S. was drought stricken. Ruin stared them in the face, and they were saved from it only by the intervention of the Federal Government. This was thru the operation of one of the most controversial measures tried by the New Deal in their efforts to mitigate the effects of the Great Depression, the program inaugurated by Henry Wallace, Secretary of Agriculture, which was popularly termed "Plowing under the Little Pigs". Perhaps no single program of the New Deal had been the subject of more acrimonious criticism.

Whether or not the economic theory behind it was valid, I do not know. I do know that this one program saved 75%, perhaps more, of the ranchmen in this country from utter ruin. With characteristic gratitude, when the rains came again and prosperity returned in 1936, most of them voted against Franklin Roosevelt!

But not Espy. Loyalty was one of his outstanding traits. He had always been nominally a Democrat, though in his early life, he had little interest in anything beyond county elections. But from this time on he became a devoted admirer of F.D.R. and of the political concepts he stood for.

This particular remedial measure was quickly implemented. Competent local cattlemen were appointed as inspectors. They made the decision on which cattle were strong enough to walk to the nearest shipping point, and which were not. The former were then shipped to the nearest packing houses, butchered, and the meat sold to the Government to be used in free meat projects all over the U.S.

Espy sold the Government 200 cows for this purpose. Those cattle too weak to walk to the railroad were shot. The Government paid $12 a head for all animals either bought or destroyed. A bulldozer dug a long pit at the ranch; the weak cattle were shot, their bodies piled into the pit and covered with quick lime and buried. I have seen few more pitiful sights in my life than those poor starving cattle lined up on the dump of that pit before their execution. That fall Espy sold his remaining calves to George Gancher of California for 3½¢ per pound for heifers and 4¢ per pound for steers.

This period was the bottom for us. Never again did we experience anything comparable to these times. The following year, 1935, was a good rainy one. The small herd that had survived the drought fattened and grew, and cattle prices began to go up. The whole experience convinced Espy that the Federal Government was his best friend. His work with the National Farm Loan Association continued.

When the Soil Conservation Service was organized in Presidio County in 1942, he was among its charter members and subsequently an enthusiastic supporter. He received in 1947 the first Conservation Award and bronze plaque from the Highland Hereford Association. For many years he had been a government weather observer and was to receive in 1957 a twenty-year pin in recognition of this service.

✦

I have mentioned before Espy's passion for junk collecting. This was a source of much embarrassment to me in the early years of our marriage, especially when he would stop at junk piles and salvage useful bits of iron, wire, pipe, etc. Eventually I also succumbed to the mania, though my collections were along slightly different lines.

Fort D.A. Russell in Marfa had been closed in the last part of President Hoover's term of Office. All of the "inspected and condemned" articles were then put up for sale by secret bids. Espy and Keesey got interested in this coming sale, made a trip to Marfa to inspect the items offered for sale, and submitted sealed bids on some of them.

The sale was held on the day early in 1933 when Roosevelt closed the banks. Everything had to be paid for in cash, and where the brothers came by the $600 in cash they spent at the sale is still a mystery to me.

They were the second highest bidders, next to some Jewish junk dealers from El Paso. They hauled many truck loads of junk home from the sale; machinery and tools of all kinds, folding theater chairs, cold scuttles, lamp shades, iron and wooden furniture, china and heavy plated silver from the hospital and many other items I have forgotten. They sold enough of the tools and machinery to repay their investment. The theatre chairs were given to the Old Baptist Church. The furniture, china, silver, etc., was gradually absorbed into our house.

Another acquisition during the 40s was the Grierson Wardrobe, which came into my possession in a roundabout way. Jimmie Livingston, a second-hand dealer in Marfa, was a friend of Espy's from whom we often made purchases. Espy had given Jimmie a piece of farm machinery, some sort of plow he no longer used, I believe. In return for this favor, Jimmie offered to give me an old wardrobe in his attic which he had bought years before from George Grierson, because, he said, I was the only person he knew whose house was big enough to hold it.

We climbed to the attic to inspect the offered gift and found it all in pieces lying scattered on the floor. But we took it nevertheless, and, as an anniversary gift, Espy sent it to the furniture repairers, DuSang's in El Paso. For $50, they restored the magnificent old piece to its original beauty. It has been the chief ornament of our house ever since. George Grierson had told Jimmie, when he bought the pieces, that his father,

General B.H. Grierson, had it hauled from Illinois to Ft. Davis in an Ox-cart in the 1880s. [33]

With the gradual improvement of our financial condition by 1935, Espy's insistence that I give up my boarders increased. Even with the most rigid economy I had barely been able to break even. Also Espy bitterly resented my working as hard as I was having to for anybody but him! Besides I was glad to be relieved of the constant job of preparing three meals a day for five extra people, as I had become pregnant again.

So early in the spring of 1935, I let the boarders go. On November 18, 1935, our third and last child, Lucy Mildred Miller, was born. She was born in our bedroom of the house in Ft. Davis, with Dr. and Mrs. Eaton in attendance.

Lucy was as perfect a baby as one could wish for. She was perfectly formed and beautiful from the moment of her birth and was always strong and healthy. She was precocious in her development and was walking and talking in sentences by the time she was nine months old. Naturally she was the center of interest in the family.

Since Clay was ten years older and Betty eight there was no problem of sibling jealousy. Instead, she was a delightful plaything for all of us. If we had not had Lucy, we would never have known what joy a baby can be, for Clay's and Betty's babyhood had been so strenuous and I had been so wretchedly unhappy during that time, that that period still remains a sort of nightmare to me. But it was different now when life had become more normal for us all.

For all our difficulties and disagreements, Espy and I were more deeply in love with every passing year. We were constantly developing more interests in common, as our children drew us closer together. Times had gotten better, and we were in easier circumstances than we had ever been before. We were drawn more and more into the many activities of the village, civic, church and social. Everything was easier and better for us except Mother, and that was a problem that would only be solved by her death twenty years later.

33 When the National Park Service restored the Commanding Officer's Quarters to its appearance during the time Colonel Benjamin Grierson and his wife Alice lived there. Daughter donated the wardrobe back to the Fort, where it resided in the front bedroom.

Espy loved children and enjoyed them hugely. His love and pride in Clay and Betty had always been inordinate, but for this adorable baby it could only be called fatuous! He loved being in the company of his children and wanted them with him at all times, whether at work or at leisure.

He considered it his duty as a father to teach them all the skills he knew, especially cowpunching. One of his strong convictions was that the training of a good cow puncher had to begin when very young. During the years we lived on the ranch and the vacation time thereafter, he was constantly "training" the children, teaching them how to ride, how to work cattle, how to care for livestock, how to do the thousand and one odd jobs necessary to running a ranch. He began when they were still so young that they did not realize they were learning, but thought it was only fun to follow their big Daddy at whatever he was doing.

I often felt that the training was entirely too strenuous and too demanding for such young children, especially the long hours in the saddle. Espy was much more rigid in his ideas of raising children (and everything else!) with the two older ones than he later became with Lucy.

Though he loved Clay and Betty devotedly, he was very strict and demanding with them and expected them to do jobs, particularly cattle work, which I felt were too great for their age and strength. This was the way that Espy had been trained as a cow puncher, and he was convinced that this was the way he should train his children. This was a continuing disagreement between us, for I felt that the development of their minds and character was far more important than learning to be expert cowpunchers. But Espy was determined to pass on to them all he knew of the various and difficult skills of a cowpuncher, with the result that both children became proficient in early youth.

This determination to impart his knowledge of and competence in ranching increased with the years, and Espy was eventually to "train" not only his own children, but his nephews, the children's friends and visitors to the ranch, and even all but the youngest of his grandchildren, who were born after his death. It would be interesting to know how many children he taught to ride horseback during his life, the number must have been legion.

One of his greatest joys was to gather a whole group of children around him on horseback and put them to work at some cowpunching task. If no urgent job existed, one could always be manufactured whenever he had a crew to work at it! He would be yelling orders at them constantly, at the top of his voice. Espy was a natural born "boss", by inheritance and inclination and training and was always prone to giving orders to everyone within the sound of his voice.

When Lucy came along, he relaxed the strict standards he had insisted on with Clay and Betty. He literally idolized the cunning baby and could see no fault in her. From the time she learned to walk she was his constant shadow. As a result, she was badly spoiled, but no baby was ever more thoroughly enjoyed.

I remember how he used to bring friends and even chance acquaintances home from town with him, just so they could admire the baby girl sunning in her basket on the South porch. Clay and Betty liked the new baby, but they were far too absorbed in their own interests to pay much attention to her. They sometimes resented the demands of a baby on their time, and the age gap was too great for them ever to develop the closeness to Lucy that they felt towards each other.

✦

In 1936 the first real sorrow of his life came to Espy in the death of his father. Mr. Miller was then 64. He was a thin, wiry man who had worked hard all of his life and had rarely been sick. In late August, he suffered a severe heart attack. Espy took him to Dr. Camp's hospital in Pecos, and stayed with him for the last three weeks of his life. From the first, Dr. Camp gave the family no hope of his recovery, and on September 20th, he died.

The fall of 1936 had been an unusually wet one. The rains had begun in August, and the dirt road to Pecos had been all but impassable even when Espy carried his father to the hospital. It had continued to rain, and it was impossible to bring the heavy hearse back from Pecos over the muddy road. So Mr. Miller's body was sent by the T&P train to Sierra Blanca, transferred to the SP train there and sent back to Marfa, then brought, with great difficulty, to Ft. Davis by hearse. This was the only time I ever heard Mrs. Miller say that she wished it would stop raining!

Watching his father suffer and die was an agonizing experience for Espy. In his own undemonstrative way, he loved his father deeply. He was crushed by grief. To see the strong man racked by sobs was a heart-breaking sight. The only love letter Espy ever wrote me was written from the hospital in Pecos, in which he told me how much he wished that I could be there to share his sad vigil. We had been married eleven years! In later years, Espy would often say that he never fully grew up until his father died. But with his wise, kind and unselfish father gone, he matured rapidly.

Mr. Miller's death brought many changes. Mrs. Miller could not continue to run the hotel without him nor manage the Union. Keesey was fully occupied with his dirt moving business and his garage. Espy was equally busy at the ranch. Audrey was teaching in Cameron. So his business interests were sold, the hotel and store to Ben Morris and his brother-in-law, Paul McWhorter, and the bank stock to others. Mrs. Miller moved back to her home, with a school teacher for company. After Audrey's marriage to Tyrone Kelly in 1938, she spent most of her time in Austin with them.

✛

The late thirties were the easiest and pleasantest years we had yet known. The financial stresses had been eased by good rains and a rising cattle market. Though we were both still working hard, we had more time to devote to civic and community affairs. With two children in school, we were drawn into all the school activities.

I was working in the Study Club, [34] PTA and the Presbyterian Church, and after the coming of Martha Holt Irving to Ft. Davis, I began to be more and more absorbed in Choral Singing. Espy was busy with the Highland Hereford, Soil Conservation Service, Federal Land Bank and West Texas Historical and Scientific Society. [35] He was elected President of the latter organization in 1936, but declined to serve as he felt unprepared to fill the office.

For the first and only time in my life, I had a full-time maid. This was Ida Silvas, daughter of the town plumber and "character" Gregorio Silvas, who came to work for me and to live with us just after Lucy was born. She lived in the little upstairs room which later became Clay's and

34 On August 20, 1924, the Fort Davis Study Club was created for the "mutual improvement in literary and social life" of the community. Mrs. Walter Miller was a founding member and once Espy and Lucy moved to Fort Davis, "Daughter" became an active member.
35 The West Texas Historic and Scientific Society was chartered in January 1926. Its permanent contribution to the region was the creation of the Museum of the Big Bend at Sul Ross State University.

she became, with her industriousness and good humor, a real help and a faithful friend. She made the trips back and forth to the ranch with us in summer, and continued to live with us until her marriage to Coco Gonzales.

Mother was an immaculate housekeeper, and she trained Ida, who, thanks to that instruction, later became the most expert cleaning woman in Ft. Davis. We were making frequent trips to El Paso, as Dr. William Chapman had begun the long ordeal of orthodontia on Clay. My cousins, Willett and Evelyn Foster, had been living in El Paso for some years, and on our trips to doctors and shopping expeditions, we always made headquarters with them.

Our circle of friends was widening and our social life becoming more active. We entertained frequently both in town and at the ranch. During the summers at the ranch, there was an almost constant stream of visitors. I have often regretted that we did not keep a guest book, so that I could remember all of the interesting people we have entertained over the years. Nearly everyone, except people who have actually lived on a ranch, seems to be completely taken in by the romanticized version of ranch life, as popularized in Western novels, movies and TV, and apparently everyone wants to visit a ranch.

Many of my relatives and Espy's came to see us. Some, like the Judge Espys, the Willett Fosters and the Zenas Bartletts came many times. The Bartletts came for a visit every summer. They were often accompanied by David Bartlett's bosom friend, "Doddy" Garrett (Dr. H. D. Garrett of El Paso). Mother's brother, Harry Conoly, spent several summers in Ft. Davis with her until his health failed.

The summers were a difficult time for Mother, for she was nervous and fearful about staying alone, and she never became reconciled to our necessary absences at the ranch. She herself never went back to the ranch after our move to Ft. Davis. Despite my uneasy conscience about leaving her alone in Ft. Davis, the summers at the ranch were a blessed respite for me from the constant tension of trying to keep peace between her and Espy. Best of all, our marriage was now on such a solid basis that nothing was ever to shake it again, though many problems remained unsolved and insoluble.

✛

One of these was religion. After Lucy was born, Clay and Betty, who had been brought up in the Union Sunday School, then held in the Presbyterian church, and to whom that beautiful old sanctuary signified the church, wanted to join the Presbyterian Church. I decided to move my membership from the Methodist to the Presbyterian Church when they did, with the hope that Espy would be willing to move his membership from the Baptist Church at the same time.

But though Espy had a strong affection for the Presbyterian Church and had grown up in it, when Mr. Bloys was the only minister in Ft. Davis, he was too much in awe of his mother, who firmly believed that the only Church was the Baptist Church, to risk offending her by becoming a Presbyterian. He did consent to hold Lucy on the day when Dr. R.L. Irving christened the baby and received Clay, Betty and me into the Church.

I have always felt that he would have been much happier if he had had the courage to go into the Presbyterian Church with me, for he was no Baptist in belief, and he had a real affection for the beautiful old Church by the mountain in which he had grown up. I am quite sure that I would have been happier, for his jealousy of my work in the church and of its members and ministers was to give me many miserable times. I used to tease him by telling him that his only religion was Anti-

Campmeeting c.1935 photo by W.D. Smithers.
Image courtesy of Fort Davis Historical Society.

Presbyterian. Yet I knew that underneath his opposition to it, his only real affection for any church was to that same Presbyterian church he was so morbidly jealous of. Espy was a contradictory personality.

For Espy, as for many people in this area, the Bloys Campmeeting stood for religion. I have heard Dr. Irving say more than once that many people in this country got so much religion during Camp Meeting that they never needed to attend a Church during the rest of the year.

This was literally true, and Espy was one of those people. He had begun attending Campmeeting as a very young child, when "Mammy" Espy had a small camp, and had later grown up in the big Finley-Jones-Espy Camp. He expected, after he married and had a family, to be asked to become a member of that camp, but we were poor relations, and the invitation did not come. Neither did Judge and Buelah Espy receive an invitation to join the Joe Espy Camp.

Some of the most uncomfortable memories I have are of days spent there in the early days of our marriage. Espy would insist on our going out to spend a day at their camp, but I have rarely felt more uncomfortable or unwanted. This exclusiveness and snobbery of the "Cow Aristocracy" as Mother scornfully called them, was much more pronounced at the period than it has since become. It was particularly characteristic of the Joe Espy tribe, who cultivated only wealthy friends and relatives.

Espy felt this slight much more keenly than I did, as their opinions were really a matter of indifference to me. We might never have become a part of the exclusive organization that Bloys Campmeeting then was, had it not been for the kindness of our dear friends Mr. and Mrs. Jesse Merrill.

Espy had known the Merrills all his life, and had grown up with their older children, and had a warm affection for both of them. I had come to know and to admire them in the Presbyterian Church. So when they cordially urged us to camp with them, we were grateful for the invitation. For some years we stayed in a tent Mrs. Merrill provided.

Later, after Keesey and Lillian bought a cabin, we stayed in one room of it. In 1940 Espy bought an old cabin from the Richard Merrills and completely rebuilt it and from then on that was our home on the camp ground.

Our relations with the Merrill family and with the Merrill Camp were among the happiest of our life. Dear, queer, Mrs. Merrill, who, as one minister's wife acutely observed **worked** at being eccentric, took a genuine liking to us, and never showed us anything but the greatest kindness. Nor did Mr. Merrill, who was one of the best men and one of the finest gentlemen I ever knew.

Mrs. Merrill had always run the camp, with the assistance of her son Richard after he grew up. When Richard died, she took Espy on in his place. They made a great team, "Emily" and Espy, and they worked together in complete harmony. They shared a conviction that early rising was one of the chief virtues. I always thought that this was the main basis of their firm friendship.

As Mrs. Merrill grew older the management of the Merrill Camp devolved more and more on Espy, a responsibility he was glad to assume, for he loved the job. Being the actual head of a camp was an extremely important "status symbol" to Espy. It put him on an equal footing with his Uncle Joe and the other "patriarchs" of Bloys Campmeeting. It also gratified his hospitable nature. Through us, the other members of the Miller family were drawn into the Campmeeting, even Mrs. Miller, who became one of the stalwarts of the Merrill Camp in her later years.

Merrill/Miller Camp, Bloys Campmeeting 2024 (Larry Francell)

Aside from the religious purpose, Bloys Campmeeting also had the best features of an old settler's reunion. It has always been the annual gathering of the widely scattered clans. Friendships were renewed and new ones made. Young people grew up, did their courting and often found their mates at the camp meeting. **36** It was also, though strictly *"sub-rosa,"* a great place for making contacts and cementing business deals.

All of these features appealed to Espy, and the Merrill Camp became one of his chief interests and pleasures in life. All children love Campmeeting and ours were no exception. Though I had at first regarded it with an extremely skeptical eye, I finally succumbed to the enduring appeal of Bloys and became a loyal member. Due to my unhappy experiences at the Espy Camp, my chief concern was that the much vaunted "wide open hospitality" should become an actuality in the Merrill Camp, and I never failed to invite every lost and lonely person I met on the campground to eat with us. **37**

Many stimulating friendships began for us at the campground, especially with various preachers, many of them became our good friends. I think especially of dear Dr. Sam Joekel, Professor of Old Testament at the Austin Presbyterian Seminary, and, because of his brilliant mind and warm personality, perhaps the most generally beloved character at Bloys for the twenty-five years he was there. He was the finest teacher I ever knew and one of the most loveable people. With that same odd attraction he had for opposites, Espy became his close friend, and to a surprising extent, his confidant.

Dr. Sam was a famous wit and story teller and the most celebrated after dinner speaker in Texas. His personal life had been tragic, but the warmth and sweetness of his personality, the brilliance of his mentality and his truly marvelous sense of humor enabled him to rise above it, and to become the scintillating center of whatever company he was in.

Those were wonderful sessions on the front porch of our cabin at Campmeeting after the night service, when Dr. Sam, Hoytt Bowles, his pupil and imitator, and others would assemble there and, before a large and admiring audience would vie with each other in telling outrageous jokes and wild yarns. Espy loved being the host to this lively crew, and enjoyed these sessions hugely.

36 "True to tradition, I met my husband at the Bloys Campmeeting." - Beth Francell
37 As long as she was able to attend, the porch of her cabin was an open invitation to one and all and was a place of lively discussion.

One of the greatest events in the history of Ft. Davis was the coming of McDonald Observatory. The two men who made the preliminary surveys which resulted in the selection of Mt. Locke, Dr. Christian Elvey, then of the University of Kansas, and a Harvard student, T.G. Mehlin came here first in the summer of 1932 and stayed at the hotel. They were here at the time we were moving into the house in Ft. Davis. Espy met them at the hotel, promptly made friends with Elvey, and brought him home to meet the family.

Elvey, who was then unmarried, was much attracted by my friend Martha Rivers Allen and courted her all during her visit to us. I have often thought how much happier both their lives would have been had she married him, as they were both unusually fine people, but she was uninterested.

As Espy was frequently in Ft. Davis that fall, and as his curiosity about and interest in the completely strange field of astronomy was vast, he took every opportunity to accompany Elvey and Mehlin on their trips to the proposed site of the observatory.

Scenic Loop road, handcolored lanternslide photo by W.D. Smithers.
Image courtesy of Fort Davis Historical Society.

The Scenic Loop [38] of 75 miles had been built just before this time, partly thru the efforts of State Senator Tom Love of Dallas, a long-time friend of the Davis Mountain Country, and partly thru the efforts of Walter Miller. Keesey has often said that his father wore out three Dodge automobiles making trips back and forth to Austin to lobby for the building of this road. The building of the Observatory on this isolated site was made possible by the existence of this excellent road.

After the site on Mt. Locke was selected, the land was donated by the Locke family, owners of the U Up & Down ranch. Contracts for the building were let. For the next four or five years, Ft. Davis saw a great deal of the builders, including Mr. H.L. Stillwell, President of Warner-Swasey Construction Co., and his various subordinates and contractors. Espy came to know all of these people and many of them became his friends. He spent much of his leisure time at the site watching the construction, and getting information from the workers about the building. They were flattered, I imagine, by his very genuine interest in their work, and his mind was expanded by contacts with them.

McDonald Observatory under construction, handcolored lanternslide photo by W.D. Smithers. Image courtesy of Fort Davis Historical Society.

38 The Scenic Loop was originally designed to be The Davis Mountains State Park Highway, the first linear state park in the nation. Promoted by State Senator Tom Love, the "park" was never established being superseded by the creation of the Davis Mountains State Park by the Civilian Conservation Corps.

This became even more true when construction was finished, and the astronomers began to arrive. The observatory was operated on a thirty-year contract between the University of Texas and the University of Chicago, by which the maintenance was the responsibility of the University of Texas and the staff was provided by the University of Chicago. Homes were built for the astronomers on Mt. Locke, they divided their time between McDonald Observatory and Yerkes Observatory at Williams Bay, Wisconsin.

Dr. Otto Struve, director of Yerkes, became the first director, and Dr. Franklin Roach the first resident astronomer. The dedication of the McDonald Observatory took place in 1939. The opening of a new Observatory which had, at that time, the third largest mirror in the world, was an event of tremendous importance in the world of astronomy. A large celebration was given by the Regents of the University of Texas, to which astronomers from all over the world were invited. The event was arranged to coincide with the 19th annual meeting for the Advancement of Science, held at Sul Ross College in Alpine on May 2, 3, 4, and 5, 1939.

This drew a large attendance of visitors, especially scientists, and featured notable speakers, a chuckwagon barbecue given by Warner Swasey Co., tours of the Big Bend area, and the actual dedication ceremonies on Mt. Locke on May 5. This last was a various gathering of world-renowned astronomers and scientists, local citizens, ranchmen and officials of the two Universities, representatives of the construction firms and, of course, the press. We had, as a house guest, Dr. Julius Olsen, Dean of Hardin-Simmons University, and a former much-loved teacher of Espy's. Espy and I were invited to all the ceremonies, which we thoroughly enjoyed. Espy immediately struck up an acquaintance with Dr. Gallo, the Mexican astronomer, thru his ability to converse with him. The principal address at the dedication was made by Dr. Struve, but the most memorable address was given the night before at Sul Ross Auditorium when Dr. Arthur H. Compton, [39] of the University of Chicago, gave the 10th John Wesley Powell lecture entitled *Physics Views the Future.*

I had gone to this largely out of curiosity to hear the famous Nobel Prize winner, with no idea that I would have much interest in or

[39] Dr. Arthur H. Compton (September 10, 1892 - March 15, 1962) won the Nobel Prize in Physics in 1927.

understanding of his lecture. To my amazement and that of the entire audience, we listened transfixed for two hours to the most profoundly stimulating talk I believe I ever heard in my life by perhaps the finest specimen of humanity I ever saw. Dr. Compton, with the vast knowledge of a scientist and the eye of a seer, sketched for his completely enthralled listeners what the recent developments of science promised for the future of the world, and warned that the beneficial discoveries might be used for the destruction rather than the betterment of humanity. His prophetic utterances were borne out all too soon by events of the coming years.

Espy was in his element during these days. He moved among these famous scientists with as much ease and confidence as though he had been one of them. Although his formal education had been poor, he had an inquiring mind and enormous curiosity about every subject under the sun. He knew nothing whatsoever of astronomy, but from the time of his first association with Elvey, he began to have a keen interest in the subject. He was not afraid to ask questions and he was not over-awed by the reputations or intellects of these famous scientists. He must have been a *"rara avis"* to them, an ignorant cowpuncher with a consuming curiosity about astronomy!

Perhaps even world-famous astronomers are intrigued by the myth of the West, or perhaps it was Espy's own special talent for friendship and his outgoing personality to which they responded, but many of them became his firm and lasting friends. These included Dr. Elvey, Dr. Struve, Dr. George Von Biesbrock and others but chiefly Dr. Gerard P. Kuiper, [40] a Dutchman who was then on the staff of the University of Chicago at Yerkes, and who became in 1957, Director of both Yerkes and McDonald Observatories.

When the 82-inch mirror was carried up the hill and installed in the dome, Espy spent the entire day on the Hill, watching the proceedings. When he returned home that night, he reported, "Mama, I've been sitting on a log all day with a pretty girl, watching them put in the telescope". The pretty girl was Sarah Fuller Kuiper, Bostonian wife

40 Gerard Kuiper (Dec. 7, 1905 - Dec. 23, 1973) A Dutch astronomer, planetary scientist and considered by many the father of modern planetary science. The Kuiper Belt is named for him. The Kuiper Belt is a circumstellar disc in the outer Solar System, extending from the orbit of Neptune.

of Gerard Kuiper. Within a few days I had met both of them, and this was the beginning of a friendship that has lasted through the years.

Other than his college chum, Tom Carson, Espy never had a closer friend than Gerard Kuiper. In spite of the differences in their background and education, there was an easy and affectionate intimacy between the two men. As I became more familiar with astronomers, the fierce professional jealousy between them became more apparent, almost as great as the jealousy between prima donnas! Perhaps one of the reasons why Gerard liked Espy was because he was not competitive, but an outsider to the profession of astronomy. Also they were both warm and friendly human beings.

I know that Gerard confided many of his professional problems and difficulties to Espy, because he felt sure of his lack of jealousy and of his sympathetic understanding. Sarah and I became equally good friends, and during the twenty years of their association with McDonald and since, close and affectionate ties existed between the two families. They were frequent visitors at the ranch during their stays in Texas, and we were often at their house on the Hill. On learning of Espy's death, Sarah told me that Gerard said that he really did not care whether he ever came back to Ft. Davis, now that Espy was gone.

Sarah came from generations of Boston "blue bloods". She laughingly told me once that her ancestors missed the Mayflower, but they came over on the next boat! She was a graduate of Smith, with keen intellectual interests and an active social conscience, and with great ease and grace of manner. She thoroughly understood the diplomatic and social role required of the wife of a world-famous astronomer and filled that role perfectly. She was constantly entertaining for house guests, close friends and visiting dignitaries, but, in keeping with her New England upbringing of "plain living and high thinking," she entertained very simply and with little apparent effort.

Stimulating conversation and an interesting exchange of ideas were Sarah's idea of a successful party, not an abundance of rich food! She was determined that we should know and enjoy the unique and interesting personalities among the astronomers as she did, and through the years she managed to introduce us to most of those who came to McDonald.

Some of these were wonderful people, like a tall old Dutchman named Mines, who was, in addition to being an astronomer, a submarine expert, and who had been the head of the Dutch underground during

World War II. At dinner at our house one night, he kept us enthralled for hours with stories of his work in hiding Jewish children from the Nazis. He was one of the most admirable human beings I ever met.

Some of the visiting astronomers were "crack-pots," like a Russian who became a real problem to get rid of. This was years later, after World War II. The man, in addition to his unpleasant personality, was a communist sympathizer. The children, who were in college then, got a big kick out of "Mama's Russian Wolf", but the experience was not funny to me.

All these contacts with people associated with McDonald were stretching Espy's horizons, but there were other broadening interests. Among these were his membership in the Highland Hereford Association and with the Marfa National Farm Loan Association, a branch of the Federal Land Bank of Houston. It was from this agency, with the help of its Secretary, Judge J.C. Fuller, that he borrowed money to buy the ranches. He became director of the Marfa National Farm Loan Association in 1936 and continued in that capacity until his death. He became deeply interested in Soil Conservation and was one of the original members of the Soil Conservation Service in this area. He put into effect so many of their recommendations on the ranch that in 1949 he was awarded the first Soil Conservation plaque given by the Highland Hereford Association.

In 1936 the Highland Hereford Association published a handsome brochure called *The Story of the Highlands*, which was illustrated by photographs made by Frank Reeves of the Ft. Worth Star Telegram. Espy accompanied Frank Reeves on many of his trips about the area to get pictures of various ranches, and often brought him to the ranch. In 1939, the Highland Hereford sponsored an auto tour of the Corn Belt feeding area. About twenty members, including Espy, made the tour. They were entertained lavishly by groups of feeders along the route. Espy's desert raised eyes feasted on the lush green farming country, with its fine crops and fat cattle. With his usual ease, he made many friends among the Midwestern feeders and buyers.

Espy received a significant honor in 1940 when he was selected as the Texas representative to make the Swift tour. During these years as a policy of advertising and of cultivating good will among cattle raisers, Swift and Co. each spring gave a three-week all expenses paid tour of their packing houses operations in Chicago, Boston, New York, Philadelphia, and Washington to a group of selected cattlemen from the cattle raising states.

Mr. Bertie Mitchell and his son, Hayes, had been the first Texans to make the tour, and in 1940 the selection fell on Espy. Espy always said afterwards that this tour made him believe in Santa Claus! It was a truly fabulous tour, under the personal supervision of one of the Swift and Co. vice Presidents, F.M. "Fanny" Simpson. The twenty or more guests were royally entertained for the three weeks, with all expenses, transportation, food, hotels, and entertainment paid by the Swift and Co. They went from their homes to Chicago, and there under Mr. Simpson's expert direction, were taken for extensive tours of all the Swift plants in these cities, and were also shown the major attractions of each city. They stayed at the finest hotels, ate in the best restaurants, and saw the leading theatrical productions.

The operation of the big meat trusts were intensely interesting to Espy. He pumped "Fanny" Simpson, and other Swift officials he met, dry on the subject. He saw and did and learned so much that was new and fascinating during those three weeks that he was always afterwards to look back on the Swift tour as the greatest thing that ever happened to him. He took a keen interest in the big cities and wanted to learn as much as possible about them.

I used to tease him about how completely Swift and Co. gained his allegiance through this wonderful trip, which was, of course, the object of the tour. "Fanny" Simpson was an astute businessman as well as a superb host, and Espy's obvious enthusiasm for the tour was probably the reason for the quick friendship that sprang up between them. He made another friend on this trip, John Beloat, a ranchman from Gila Bend, Arizona. The only incident to mar the perfection of the trip was the sudden death from illness, near the end of the it, of one of the members.

Espy had stayed at home so closely for so many years that he was almost afraid to undertake the journey when the offer first came. I had to encourage him and push him to get him off on it, but once started, he got more pleasure and benefit from the tour than anyone who ever took it, I feel sure. Espy had tremendous zest for living and unlimited curiosity about people and places. This trip whetted his desire for travel. New York City had impressed him most of all, and he always afterwards wanted to take me to New York and show me its wonders. This trip enormously stimulated his eagerness to see new and different parts of the country. Though we had never had enough money to take many trips, he dearly loved traveling. Nor was he one of those who travel to confirm his prejudices, for he learned from every trip he made and from every person he met.

Just prior to his departure on the Swift tour, we found out, through examinations by Dr. C.E. Eaton in Ft. Davis, and Dr. Jim Camp in Pecos, that Espy had developed diabetes. This was an hereditary tendency in the Espy family, many of whose members, including Mr. Joe, had the disease, but Espy only developed it after he became so greatly overweight.

It was a shattering blow to the big strong man, who had always prided himself on his health and vigor, to learn that he had a chronic disease with which he would have to live for the rest of his life. He was always to regard diabetes as faintly disgraceful. He never wanted anybody to know that he was a diabetic, though naturally his restricted diet and dependence on daily shots of insulin were obvious proof of it.

From 1940 on he was under continual treatment to control the diabetes from a succession of doctors; Dr. Eaton, Dr. Camp, Dr. Chester Awe of El Paso, and, finally, Don Gaddis of Ft. Davis. In spite of their constant efforts to control the disease, he was never able for the remaining twenty years of his life, to do without insulin. He learned to give himself the daily shots and to make urine tests, and submitted to the restriction of the disease with surprising good grace. Being deprived of sweets was the greatest hardship, for he loved sweets and never got over craving them.

At the insistence of the doctors, he would go on rigid diets periodically, and did succeed in pulling 20 or 25 pounds off his peak weight of 240. But it was an everlasting struggle to get the weight off and to keep it off, and eventually he came to depend more on the increasing dosage of insulin than on diet to keep the diabetes under control. Dr. Camp told him, when he first discovered that he had diabetes, that it would shorten his life by twenty years. I am sure that it did, for physically Espy was very like his mother, who lived to be 88, while he died at 64.

The summer before Lucy was born, Espy had to have his tonsils removed, no minor operation for a man of 40. Keesey and I took him to the old Masonic Hospital in El Paso. I was seriously worried about his ability to stand the operation. It was a bad one, and his subsequent hemorrhaging frightened even Keesey, but again his strong constitution pulled him through. The diabetes had not yet developed and except for the fact that overweight was slowing him down considerably, he was apparently as strong and robust as before. Even after he developed diabetes, he made no concessions to the disease other than in diet and insulin shots, and continued to do the strenuous work of a cowpuncher as he had most of his life.

Probably the most important event in this period of Espy's life was the purchase of the Miller Ranch. He had had chances in earlier years to buy ranches in the vicinity, the Bob Bell place, a small place on the highway near the stock pens, now owned by "Slim" Brown, and the Foley Ranch, now owned by the Roosevelts. [41] After due consideration, he had decided against buying either, as they had poor turf and were subject to drought, but he had long cast speculative glances at the Kimball Ranch, which joined his country on the West. It was desirable land and blocked well with what he already owned.

The late thirties had been prosperous one for the ranch industry, with good rains and fair prices. Our expenses were also growing heavier as our family grew older. Like all old-time cattlemen, Espy always wanted more land. There were two reasons for this, their natural land hunger, or greed!, and the fact that land has always represented the best and almost the only investment for cattlemen. A ranchman could always borrow money on land and their credit rating deepened chiefly on the amount of land they owned.

But even more important than that, land was a status symbol. A man's wealth and importance were gauged by the number of sections he owned or controlled. Before the discovery of oil and gas on West Texas ranches, few cattlemen had any other source of income than land and cattle. In addition to this pride of possession and though they might be

41 Al Roosevelt and his family later were close friends of Clay and Jody Miller and frequent visitors to the ranch. Al was quick to claim kinship with Teddy Roosevelt, but not Franklin.

hopelessly in debt to the bank or loan sharks, they still regarded themselves as "Masters of all they surveyed" if their cattle grazed on wide acres. In their well-worn clothes and rundown boots, they felt themselves to be lords of the earth, different from (and better than!) the ordinary run of men. This I believe, is the secret "mystique" of the cowboy and ranch legend in American folklore, literature and stage, and the main reason for the enduring fascination that legend exerts.

In early years, the struggle for land in this country had been a constant source of trouble between ranchmen themselves, between ranchmen and their natural enemies, sheepmen and farmers, and even between ranchmen and governments. Ranchmen generally were a high-handed bunch, who tended to take the law in their own hands, on occasion. Many and bloody had been the struggles over land even in this country in the 1870s and 1880s. But fortunes were no longer built on free range, since the advent of barbed wire, and for many years the only way a man could acquire land out here was by purchase, inheritance or marriage.

Many a ranchman "went broke" trying to buy enough land to set up each of his sons in the cattle business. One of the best chances an ambitious young cowpuncher had of acquiring a ranch was to marry the daughter of a rich ranchman, as Joe Espy had done. Espy had had these chances, too, but had not taken any of them. In later years, when rich oil men, doctors and corporations began investing their surplus wealth in ranch lands, both because status still attaches to owning a ranch and because a ranch is a good losing investment, the story is different. But at the time of Espy's entry into the cattle business, he was the only man of his generation in this area who neither inherited nor married his land. He was unique in that he bought his land, and held on to it all of his life.

So when Otis Kimball of Alpine, Keesey's life long friend, who had bought the ranch joining us on the West from the Van Neills some ten years earlier, decided to sell it and concentrate his ranch holdings in Brewster Co., he offered the ranch to Keesey. Keesey, in addition to his garage business in Ft. Davis, had for some years been in partnership with Arthur Babcock, a former highway engineer, in a very successful dirt moving business.

After much discussion, Espy and Keesey decided to pool their resources and buy the Kimball place. Espy had no cash to pay for his half of the purchase, so he obtained a second loan of $112,000 from the Federal Land Bank. Since he had already borrowed the maximum amount the bank allowed on one loan, the new loan was made in the name of his wife, Lucy Foster Miller. From this circumstance, a rumor started in Marfa that Espy paid for his half of the Kimball ranch with his rich wife's money!

The Kimball ranch consisted of 16,000 acres and was bought for $7 an acre. Thus Keesey and I became (on paper!) joint owners of what has been called from then on the Miller Ranch. Keesey was fully occupied with his other interests, so Espy assumed the management of the new ranch along with his own, though, for reasons of economy, he was paid no salary. The brothers also purchased the cattle with which the ranch was stocked.

That fall, Espy made a trip to the W.L. Kokernot ranches, southeast of Alpine, and bought their calf crop. In spite of the disastrous experience that Espy and Den Knight had previously had with sheep, they decided to stock sheep on the ranch, as sheep offered more and quicker profits. About 4,000 sheep were purchased in August of 1940 and moved to the Miller Ranch. Bob Dod, a cowpuncher who had run the ranch for Otis, stayed on at the Miller Ranch and worked for us for a number of years. The addition of sheep greatly increased Espy's work and responsibilities, as they require more attention and care than cattle do.

Also, we were soon to learn, they are far more vulnerable than cattle, subject to a wide variety of diseases and the natural prey of many predators. The sheep had no sooner gotten on the ranch than the predators, coyotes, bobcats, eagles and mountain lions, discovered them, and from then on it was incessant warfare against the "Varmints". We had not known there were mountain lions on the ranch until the sheep came, but they soon began their depredations, killing sheep wantonly for fun, as well as to eat.

Espy enlisted the help of government hunters and trappers, Fred Moore with his highly intelligent bunch of hounds and Nelson Elliott, a skilled trapper. The panther hunts were highly exciting and Espy thoroughly enjoyed them. They reminded him of the bear hunts he had taken part in as a boy. About a dozen of the huge cats were killed on the ranch during the years we had sheep, besides many bobcats and coyotes. I hesitate to tell it, because of our son's subsequent part in the protection of the Golden Eagle, but Espy hired a professional hunter, Casparis, to hunt eagles from a plane.[42]

Sheep shearing was another exciting time. The sheep did well that first year. In spite of losses to disease, cold and predators there were 120 lambs, an 80% crop. In May the shearers came, and during the time they were there, every available person on the ranch was put to work gathering and holding sheep for the shearers, marking lambs, and reuniting them with their mothers. Even Lillian and I were pressed into service to cook for the men, although the shearing crew had its own cook.

During the early 40s, Espy did much soil conservation work on the ranch, building dumps and dams to divert the force of the summer flood waters, experimenting with various types of grass, resting pastures and clearing off the prickly pear. The later work was done by immigrant Mexican labor, which was almost the only sort available then. The Northern Mexican states were suffering from one of their frequent periods of drought, and abnormally large numbers of immigrants were coming into the U.S. in search of work. The Vieja trail through ZH Canyon was one of their favorite routes into the country. We had always made a practice of feeding any of the weary travelers who stopped at our gates. They had already walked 18 miles from the river, probably much more, and were always hungry, ragged and foot sore. Often rude sandals cut from an old inner tube would be their only foot covering. So we always gave them food and sometimes work.

When the Soil Conservation Service began to pay ranchmen for clearing the land of prickly pear, Espy would hire groups of them to do the cutting, sometimes only a few, sometimes there were thirty or forty at work on the place at one time.

They lived in rude camps in the mountains, to which he hauled food and water. It was illegal to hire them, [43] and the immigration officers were constantly searching for aliens, for practically all the ranchmen were using immigrant labor. As fast as the "Chotas" [44] caught the immigrants and carried them back to Mexico, they would slip back

42 John Casparis, for whom the airport in Alpine is named, was infamous for shooting flying eagles, and coyotes on the ground, from the cockpit of his airplane.
43 "Until about 1970 it was not illegal to hire "undocumented" immigrants or workers." Clay Espy Miller, Jr.
44 "Chotas" Border Patrol Agents

across the river to work in the U.S. again. The constant "cat and mouse" game with the "chotas" made hiring them hazardous, for ranchmen never new knew when the officers might appear and search their premises for immigrants. Sometimes they found them and hauled them off, but the immigrants were very clever at hiding themselves at the first approach of a strange vehicle. Many were the wildly exciting chases that took place on the ranches, but they were usually good natured, for we felt that even though the "chotas" were trying to enforce the law, their sympathies were with the poor hungry aliens, as ours were. After all, it was war time, and ours was a great meat producing area. Since all the able-bodied young men, Anglo and Latin both, had gone to war, the ranch business could not have been carried on without the aid of the immigrants.

The workers had to be paid, of course, in cash. When he had large groups of men working at the pear cutting, Espy would bring home a big roll of bills from the bank in Fort Davis, and hide it somewhere around the house until payday arrived. Once, when he had done this, he lost a roll containing $600. After a frantic search, it was finally discovered under the cushions of the davenport. I have often thought since of what a risk he ran, when he would sit down on the side of a hill with a big group of immigrants, most of whom he'd never seen until a few days or weeks before, take out his wad of cash and begin to pay them off. He had no way of knowing whether there might be thieves or murderers among them who would kill him for the money. But he never had the least trouble with any of them, perhaps because he was fair to them. It never seemed to occur to him that he was taking any special risk.

Another instance of his coolness and courage in face of danger occurred during the war years, when two men, both of whom had been working for him, got into a fight on our back porch and began slashing at each other with knives. Espy waded in between them, flailing them with his arms, and yelling at them in Spanish, until he had them separated. Then he hauled the one who had started the fight off to town. It is remarkable, too, that with all the strange men who worked on the ranch over the years, there was so little theft. I recall only two instances. Once some young boys who had been working in the yard, broke into the house and stole a pair of spurs. Another time one of the men working at the farm tried to steal a pickup and was promptly reported by another worker and caught.

Those were busy years before World War II and generally prosperous ones, and usually with adequate rainfall. Our children were rapidly growing up and we were more and more involved in their interests and in civic and community affairs. The "Day of Infamy", December 7, 1941, shocked us, as it did the whole nation, out of our ease and complacency. Immediately war time restrictions on rubber, gas, food and shoes began to be imposed. Espy bought a new Dodge Sedan just before Pearl Harbor, which we drove for the next six years. That Christmas we decided to go back to Marlin for the Conoly family reunion at the home of the Zenas Bartletts, as it was apparent that traveling would soon be rigidly curtailed by lack of gas and tires. I have always been thankful that we did go back for the last happy reunion with my beloved family, for the following December dear Uncle Zenas died, and there were never any more reunions.

Because ranching was an essential industry, we got sufficient gasoline for our needs, though there was no driving for pleasure. In later years, I realized that gas rationing was a lucky break for us, with two teen agers. As a result of it, we had no problems about their driving. Espy had taught them both to drive when young, as he always tried to teach them every skill he knew. But all driving was then strictly for business.

The other shortages did not inconvenience us greatly. We got brown Mexican sugar from Ojinaga by the 100 lb. sack, which enabled us to preserve our fruit crops. Espy was a hoarder by nature. He got worried about a possible shortage of toilet paper, and bought two huge cartons of it from the Union [45] and stored them in "Jim's" room at the ranch. When the war was over and we finally needed it, we found that termites had gotten into the cartons and had eaten most of the toilet paper! Espy took considerable ribbing about his hoarding as a result of this.

We were doing our part toward the war effort. Espy was investing every dollar he could into War Savings Bonds. I was working in Red Cross and first aid classes. Fort Davis mothers were also taking groups of Fort Davis girls, heavily chaperoned, to dances given for the

---

[45] The Union Mercantile in Fort Davis, owned then by Tyrone Kelly.

young Cadets at the Air Force Base in Marfa and on week-ends, we usually had large groups of these lonely boys for visitors. My homemade grape juice and cookies supplied refreshments. The labor shortage was the greatest problem for ranchmen during the war and was only partly alleviated by the use of immigrant labor.

+

Sometime during the spring of 1943, Espy suffered a bad accident while riding in the mountains. He always said that his horse sat down on him. What really happened was that the horse reared up and fell over backwards with him, and severely injured his right knee. He managed somehow to get back on the horse and to ride back to the house, though he was in agony from the pain. Doctors were in scarce supply during the war years. The only available one was at the Marfa Air Force Base. He X-rayed the knee and found that it was not broken, and advised massage. Espy made regular trips to the Base Hospital for treatments by a professional masseur, but the knee continued to be weak and painful. He was so badly crippled from it that it was often hard for him to walk at all. But, in a mistaken idea that constant use would eventually "limber it up", he continued to work and ride as usual, for he had no help on the ranch except an occasional laborer.

Clay graduated from Fort Davis High School in 1943. We knew that he would have to go into the service when he was 18, and wanted him to get as much education as possible before that time arrived. Immediately after his graduation, we put the little 16 year old country boy on a bus for Lubbock to enter Texas Tech. The colleges were then on an accelerated schedule, and were running full twelve months, because of the war.

Clay found a second home in Lubbock in that of his great-uncle "Bud," brother of Walter Miller, and his wife, Aunt Tine, and became a member of their family. Later he moved into their hospitable home, and in return for milking the cow and doing the chores, enjoyed their welcome company and Aunt Tine's good cooking. That fall, the youngest son of the family, Captain Jim Miller, was lost when his plane went down over the North Sea. When Clay came home at Christmas, he told us of his decision to enlist in the Air Corps, and he brought with him a waiver for us to sign, since he still lacked six months of being 18.

It was a cruelly hard decision for Espy and me to make, for the war was at its most discouraging depths just then with no ray of hope for its ending. But Clay was determined, and we signed the waiver, and he enlisted in the Air Corps on his return to Lubbock in January 1944. Fortunately for us, the tide of the war began to turn soon after. Clay's class of prospective pilots (19,000 of them) were not called up for almost a year, did not receive flight training and got an early discharge. Meanwhile he was able to complete two years of college work at Tech before his call to the Air Force finally came.

When Clay went off to college, Espy lost his best help. He had only 15-year-old Betty, who was, however, a competent cowhand and a Mexican man named George to depend on, as he himself was still too crippled to do much. Just then a letter came from a friend he had made on the Swift Tour, Fred Henderson of Camden, Alabama, asking Espy if he would let Fred's 16-year-old nephew, Jimmie Henderson, come out and work on the ranch that summer.

By then Espy was grasping at straws for help, and he wrote Fred to send the boy. I was much opposed to the idea, for I expected him to be a spoiled and lazy brat, used to having Negroes wait on him hand and foot. But I was wrong, for Jimmie proved to be a real help. He was a bright sweet-tempered fellow, as industrious as could be and eager to learn all about the ranch business in three months' time! He fit easily and pleasantly into the family circle, and he provided an unending source of entertainment with his tales of plantation life and his deep Southern accent. That summer, Jimmie, Betty and George did the work on the ranch under Espy's supervision. We came to be genuinely fond of Jimmie. At Christmas time I still get cards from him, with pictures of the "pretty woman," with who he was already in love, and their four fine children.

In 1944, after disposing of his interests in the garage business and in the dirt moving partnership, Keesey moved to Dallas to take a job with the Smaller War Plants Corporation. The brothers decided to lease the Miller Ranch, due to the labor shortage and Espy's crippled condition. In June 1944, they leased the Miller Ranch to Reuben Keys and Worth Evans for two years. Reuben and Worth promptly overstocked it, as they did all their ranches, resulting in serious damage to the turf.

Keesey was unhappy in the big city of Dallas, though Lillian thoroughly enjoyed it, and, at the end of a year, the family returned to

Fort Davis. Keesey began at once to take more responsibility at the Miller Ranch. He moved a small trailer house out here, where he could "batch" and where Lillian and K.K. could stay on weekends and during the summer. Ciquel Gonzales and his family were then living in the old house on the Miller Ranch. Later it was occupied by Denny Baldwin, Mrs. Denny (Minnie) and their boys Virgil, Allen, and Mike. Denny worked for the brothers until after Clay's return to the ranch.

Betty graduated from High School in 1944 and went off to school at TSCW (Texas State College for Women) in Denton that fall with her friend Nellie Barnett of Valentine. Espy carried the two little country girls to Pecos and put them on the TP train for Denton. Betty recalls that they were so fearful of losing their money that neither could sleep during the long night on the Pullman. She spent two years at TSCW before transferring to the University of Texas in her Junior year. Clay continued his studies at Tech through the summer of 1945, thus completing two full years of college work.

Towards the end of her second year at TSCW, Betty wrote me that she had met a little girl at school whom she thought Clay would like, and that she wanted to bring home for a visit. I consented, of course, and she brought her friend, Jo Ellen Canada, always called Jody, of Tulsa, Oklahoma, home for a visit at the end of school. And Betty had judged correctly for from the minute Clay laid eyes on the diminutive little girl – she was four foot nine and weighed 95 pounds!, he knew that she was the one he wanted. I recall that the courtship went on that summer as he plowed the garden south of the house with a tractor – with Jody sitting on the rack watching him. It continued steadily through the rest of his years in school, but strong minded little Jody refused to marry him until she had gotten her degree in Physical Education from TSCW, and had taught for a year in a college.

Clay did not return to Tech for the fall semester, as he was expecting his call from the Air Force momentarily. It came in January. He was sent first to Keesler Field, near Biloxi, Mississippi, and was later transferred to Roswell, New Mexico. We made a trip to Roswell in the summer of '46 to see him. Since his class of Air Force Volunteers had never received pilot training, due to the improvement in War Conditions, he was doing clerical work at the Roswell base in an office with a group of Negro WACs [46] from Chicago working as stenographers for him. In

------

[46] WAC, Women's Army Corps, created in 1942 as an auxiliary of the U.S. Army.

November 1946 he received his discharge, and went back to Tech in January 1947, and stayed through the summer term. That fall he and Betty both transferred to the University of Texas, Clay received his B.A. degree there in June 1948. Betty did not graduate as she married Leon Geddis Byerley Jr. of Midland, whom she met soon after entering the University in April 1948.

In the summer of 1948, Dr. Frank Blair, head of the Zoology Department at the University of Texas and Clay's good friend, brought his class of 24 graduate students, of whom Clay was one, to the ranch for a six week course of study of the fauna of the region. They camped in the mess hall at Old Camp Holland in Vieja Canyon, and spent their time trapping, collecting and preserving zoological specimens. They were an interesting bunch of boys and Espy greatly enjoyed them, though he never got used to the casual manner in which the herpetologists among them handled snakes. It also bothered him to see lights appearing suddenly at any part of the ranch during the nights. It was only boys settling or checking their traps, but it disturbed his rest considerably. Espy was thoroughly saturated with all the fears and prejudices of the pioneer ranchmen, who always looked with suspicion on the advent of any stranger on their territory, especially at night! This was the result of the prevalence of cattle thieves in the earlier days in this country. All of his life Espy was accustomed to try to account for the tracks of every strange vehicle, horse or pedestrian that appeared anywhere on the ranch, and any tracks that could not be reasonably accounted for were open to suspicion.

That fall Clay took a job with the Texas Fish and Game Commission trapping surplus antelope in the Trans-Pecos Region and transferring them by truck to other locations. He planned to return to the University of Texas at the beginning of the Spring Semester in 1949 and complete work on his M.A. degree in zoology. It was his intention to make a career as a zoologist, probably in government service. Near the end of January 1949 one of the most severe snow storms this country had ever seen occurred.

Temperatures plunged far below zero, and heavy snow made roads virtually impassible. Clay was living alone in a tent way below Marathon, miles from any neighbor. As temperatures dropped and the snow grew heavier, we became more and more worried about the danger Clay was in, for reports of death by freezing were frequent over the radio. When the thermometer stood at 14° one morning, we could endure the suspense no longer, and Espy and Keesey started out in a pickup equipped with chains to hunt for Clay. They found him on the highway, miles from nowhere, repairing a flat tire, his fingers and ears already frostbitten, and brought him safely home. Next morning after food and a hot bath and a good night's sleep, he came down into the kitchen and stared out at the snowy landscape. The thermometer rested on 0°, but the snow had stopped falling. "This plays heck with my plans," he remarked to me. I remonstrated that the spring session at the University did not open for several days yet. "Oh, yes, but I was going to Missouri today," he replied. Jody was then teaching at Cattey College in Nevada, Missouri. And go to Missouri he did, leaving at noon that same day, in spite of our pleas not to start out in such weather. A couple of days later he wired us from Nevada, "a hard trip but worth it!"

After the expiration of the lease to Evans and Keyes in 1946, the Miller brothers took back the Miller ranch and began trying to repair the damage done to the turf by two years of "sheeping". This necessitated Keesey spending more and more time at the ranch.

In 1948, just ten years after their purchase of the Miller ranch, the brothers bought that portion of the Old Foley ranch which joined us on the West. This consisted of 5860 acres, and was bought for $11.75 an acre, or $67,500. This piece of country blocked in neatly with their existing land and brought the combined acreage of the three ranches to around 27.4 sections. Espy continued to operate his own ranch, which we now began calling "La Vieja" after the mountain pass behind it, while he and Keesey jointly operated the Miller and Foley ranches, henceforth called simply the Miller Ranch, as a unit. Most operational expenses, cattle sales, etc., were handled jointly in a loose partnership arrangement.

Espy's civic duties were increasing as well as his responsibility on the ranch. He had helped organize the Soil Conservation Service in Presidio Co., in 1940 and served as Chairman of the Board of Supervisor for two five-year terms. He was awarded the first plaque given by the Highland Hereford Association for outstanding work in Soil Conservation. He had also been on the Board of Directors of the Highland Hereford Association for years, and served for two years (1948-50) as President of that Organization. He was a member of the

Board of Directors of the Marfa National Farm Loan Association from the early forties until his death and made many trips to Houston to attend meetings of the Federal Land Bank.

He had a close personal friend and admirer in Barry Scobee, historian and publicity agent par excellence for Ft. Davis. Barry constantly pumped Espy for material for news stories about the history of the area and for news of the cattle business and used him as a source for dozens of these stories. It was during this period that his picture appeared frequently in West Texas newspapers. Some years later when he met an old friend (Viola Ward of Pecos) whom he had not seen in some years, she remarked, "Well, Espy, I thought you must be dead! I hadn't seen your picture in the papers in the last few weeks!"

Our first grandchild, Ruth Elizabeth Byerley, was born December 11, 1948. From then on Espy had a new and absorbing interest in life – grandchildren! Leon had transferred to the University of California the preceding fall. In March Espy, Lucy and I made a trip to California to see the new member of the family. We spent a week in Berkley with our children, during which we did considerable sightseeing in and around San Francisco. Espy was considerably more impressed with this fascinating city than he had been on his first acquaintance with it in his days in the Navy in World War I. We drove out to California by way of Grand Canyon [47] and returned down the scenic coastal highway to San Diego, where we visited with Leon's Aunts (his mother's sisters) Mrs. Mary Anderson, Mrs. Esther Robbins, and Mrs. Grace Gray, before returning home by the Southern Route.

Espy loved traveling and had unbounded curiosity about new places and people. He never saw a new road that he did not want to explore it, and he rarely saw a stranger without trying to strike up an acquaintance with him. I always expected to see somebody "beat his ears down" for his uninhibited intrusions into their privacy, but no one ever did. On the contrary, all sorts of people seemed to enjoy his bluff friendliness and easy Western manners.

Traveling with him was always a lively and interesting experience, but it was often a harrowing one as well, for his driving was

---

47 "And Harrods Casino in Las Vegas." Lucy Miller Jacobson calculated to shake the strongest nerves. He was an expert driver but an erratic one. He had the Western habit of driving down the center of the road. It was safer there, he always explained, when you had a blowout. What happened when you met another car was something else, but of course you did not meet so many cars when Espy began to drive. I have seen him do amazing feats of quick thinking and instantaneous action in a car, thereby averting what looked like a certain collision. He expected a car, particularly a pickup, to do anything a horse would do.

I have suffered agonies of nervousness and fear as we bumped and bounced all over the ranch, regardless of the roughness of the terrain. For he always wanted my company on his frequent trips to far corners of the ranch. Why, I don't know, for he knew how I hated driving over that rough country! But I often had to, nevertheless. As he grew older and spent more and more years incessantly commuting between the ranch and Ft. Davis, he grew more and more careless in his driving and I grew steadily more afraid of it. He was indignant at my nervousness, for he considered himself a fine driver; he often reminded me that he had never had a serious accident. This was true, but there is no telling how many I saved him from by screaming out just in time! His driving became notorious all over the country, especially his habit of reading a newspaper propped against the steering wheel as he drove down the middle of the road!

In June 1949 we made another trip, this time to Nevada, Missouri to attend the wedding of Jody and Clay. Clay had driven up from Austin, where he was in graduate school, with his cousin, K.K. who was to be his best man. Jody presided over the graduation ceremonies of her class at noon, and at five o'clock on June 5th was married in a very formal and impressive ceremony at the beautiful little Episcopal Church in Nevada. The cherubic little priest, Father Foland, was attired in the most dazzling scarlet and gold robes. I remarked afterwards to Jody that it was the only wedding I ever attended where the priest outshone the bride! But the little bride was beautiful, too, in an exquisitely simple dress her mother had made.

Clay and Jody left immediately after the ceremony for Austin. K.K. drove Espy, Lucy and me home, and for once I enjoyed the luxury of a good chauffeur! How I did enjoy that drive home thru the gloriously green Ozark Mountains! K.K. was also accommodating. He told his mother later that he "never got out of low gear on the whole trip, because Daughter had him stop at every antique and junk shop."

Espy and Keesey had often discussed the possibility of drilling deep wells along the course of Wild Horse Draw and of striking a stream of water of sufficient volume for irrigation. This area in Aeons past was the bottom of an inland sea, and they and many others had long suspected that an abundant water supply probably lay underneath it.

In July 1949 they had an exploratory well put down and, at a depth of 420 feet, struck a fine stream of water. This made possible their dream of putting part of their land under cultivation. They called in the help of experts from the Soil Conservation Service to level the land and lay it off for irrigation. By the use of big machinery Keesey had brought to the ranch, the work of laying off fields, ditches, and dumps was begun, and as soon as they finished, grass crops were planted.

This had an unforeseen result. In August Clay and Jody came home from Austin on a visit. Espy immediately took them down to see the new well. Clay stood for a long time gazing at the life-giving stream of water pouring out of the ground, and apparently without a regret, discarded his cherished ambition for a career as a zoologist and decided to come back home and run a farm irrigated by this water. Jody, perfect wife that she has always been, acquiesced in his decision, and, city-bred though she was, eventually made the best ranchman's wife I ever knew. At the end of the summer, they returned to the ranch. To my great disappointment, Clay's Master's Degree, which lacked only writing the theses, was never completed. If Clay or Jody ever regretted this decision to return to the ranch, no one has ever known of it.

The old house on the Miller ranch was occupied at that time by Denny Baldwin and family. But there was a three room house at the foot of Indian Point Canyon about five miles from the farm. This was cleaned up and put in repair, and a bath, second bedroom and living room added. As soon as it was finished, Clay and Jody moved there from the Vieja. Their first son, Albert Walter Miller, was born June 9, 1950.

A second well was dug on the Miller ranch in 1951 and more acres were put under cultivation. "The farm" of some 400 acres, as this part of the ranch came to be called, soon became the center of operations.

Huge dirt tanks were built near each well to impound the water as it was pumped. Fields were laid off and ditches dug to carry the irrigation water, all under Soil Conservation supervision. Some of the fields were planted with a mixture of grasses for permanent pasture, to be used for winter grazing, and others were planted with Alfalfa and Hegira. [48] It was a never ceasing matter of astonishment to me that summer to watch the phenomenal growth of the latter crop. I never stopped marveling at the lush fields of tall waving green stalks. Verily, the irrigation wells had made the desert "to blossom like the rose".

During the summer K.K. dug a huge pit silo at the farm with the big cat. In fall, when the heavy heads of grain were ripe, the hegira was harvested with a recently purchased ensilage cutter and stored in the pit silo for winter use. The harvesting operation was fascinating to watch. Clay drove the ensilage cutter slowly down the rows of tall stalks; the coarse stalks and grain were cut up into pieces no longer than an inch in length by the machine, and were blown, thru a spout at the rear, into the bed of a dump truck following behind the ensilage cutter. As soon as one dump truck was filled, it raced to dump its load into the pit silo, while another truck took its place, to receive its load in turn. A small tractor ran back and forth constantly over the freshly cut silage in the pit, packing it down and converting it into food for cattle during the winter.

Building was constantly going on at the farm. Feedlots were built in which the animals to be fed were kept. A trough ran around the outside of each of these, and into this a truck, called a HYLex, poured a stream of the cured silage morning and evenings. A large Quonset hut was erected near the first well for a shop and storage barn for machinery. The brothers were constantly buying bigger and better machinery, so there were soon too many vehicles for the barn and they were parked all over the area. Bunk houses were built for the Mexican laborers at the farm. The work of farming went on simultaneously with the ranch work, and was done under the supervision of Espy, Keesey and Clay, each taking primary responsibility for the field he was best fitted for, Espy for the cattle, Keesey for the machinery and Clay for the farming. The three men worked in astonishing harmony, considering that they were all hard-headed Millers!

---

48 Hegira is a variety of sorghum, a type of grain, used for cattle feed.

The farm proved its value to their cattle operation during the Long Drought, 1946 to 1957, [49] as the feed it produced, under irrigation, saved the Miller brothers from going broke as so many cattlemen in the Big Bend/Davis Mts. area did. Even aside from the drought, it proved a valuable asset, both socially and financially. Its verdant fields were one of the show places of the area. Visitors came from far and near to see them and to study their operation. The brothers successful experiment was the subject of several articles in ranch and Soil Conservation publications. Clay early stocked both storage tanks with perch and bass, and as these multiplied, they attracted the fishermen among our friends and neighbors.

Visitors, other than human, were attracted by the green fields, for the mule deer, natives of the area, soon discovered them and began invading them in constantly increasing numbers. I cannot recall exactly what year it was that Espy began to have paid hunters on the ranch, though I have a vivid recollection of the scorn local ranchmen heaped on the Fowlkes brothers, in the early years of my marriage, when they first began the practice of taking hunters for **PAY!** Before then, ranchmen *invited* special friends to hunt, or people they wished to impress or influence. Within a very few years after the Fowlkes boys initial venture in "selling deer;" however, most of the ranchmen in the area were following their example. In due time they became thankful for this additional source of revenue, and they came to regard their deer as a crop to be harvested.

An accidental meeting on the highway with a car full of hunters resulted in Espy's leasing the ranch for deer hunting purposes to them. This group was made up of dedicated hunters from deep East Texas, woodsmen all and deadshots. Most of them were prosperous rice farmers but the leader of the group, as long as he lived, was a successful contractor from Liberty, Elmer Ratcliff. Espy and Elmer became good friends. This group, with varying membership, leased hunting rights on the ranch for more than twenty years. The constantly increasing numbers of deer, attracted from a wide territory to our green fields, gradually became a more and more profitable source of revenue on the ranch, though our nervousness over the "trigger happy" (and often drunk!) hunters tended to mitigate our pleasure in this source of profit.

49 According to Clay Espy Miller, Jr., the years 1950 to 1958 were the worst.

During the years since the original accident, the injury to Espy's knee had grown steadily worse. By the summer of 1951, he was walking with a cane and had to have help to get on his horse. In spite of this, in June of that year, Espy, Lucy and I made a short trip up into Colorado. We drove up the Eastern side, and visited with my aunt, Mrs. W.E. Bradford, and Espy's cousin, Chandler Prude, in Denver, then went on to Estes Park and came down the Western slope. In spite of the constant pain in his knee, Espy thoroughly enjoyed the magnificent scenery, though I think he was as scared as I was on that hazardous stretch between Ouray and Silverton, then known as "the million-dollar highway." [50]

We went on to Mesa Verde Park and walked along the trails to the cliff dwellings, where an amusing incident happened. Espy was naturally an imposing figure and in well tailored slacks, white shirt and tie, and a beautiful broad brimmed Panama hat, he was really impressive, and in vivid contrast to the motley attire of the other tourists. As he walked slowly along, aided by his cane, a pleasant young man asked him, solicitously, "Can I be of any help to you, Colonel?"

The driving during this trip did not help the knee trouble. It grew steadily worse until he could no longer walk. For some years Espy had been a patient of Dr. Chester Awe of El Paso, a specialist in diabetes. We took Espy to El Paso, where Dr. Awe put him in the hospital for ten days and treated him with an experimental drug, adrenal cartes, [51] thinking perhaps his trouble was arthritis. This was no improvement, so he called in consultation a bone specialist, Dr. David Cameron, who advised an immediate operation on the knee. The operation, for what is commonly called "football knee", was performed and while it was not the most dangerous of Espy's several operations, it was probably the most painful. Dr. Cameron told me that he had performed this operation hundreds of times, but that Espy's knee was in the worst condition he had ever seen, with the cartilage so torn that it looked "like grains of rice." Espy had unwittingly done much of this damage himself, in his mistaken effort to force the stiffness out of the knee joint by constant use.

50 In 1951 the "Million Dollar Highway" was still unpaved, and was called that because the gravel base on the road was from area mine "tailings" that were still considered to have gold.
51 Adrenal corticosteroids were developed during the 1930s-1950s as a treatment for inflammation.

Dr. Cameron gave us no hope that, with the complication of diabetes, Espy would ever walk again. The pain he endured in the weeks following the operation was excruciating, especially when the doctors drew off the surplus fluid from the knee with needles. Poor Espy would grip the rungs at the top of his bed with his hands, and clinch his teeth to keep from crying out in agony, while sweat poured off his face.

Slowly the knee began to mend and he grew better. After several weeks in the hospital the heavy cast was removed, and I was allowed to take him home. He was on crutches for several months, then graduated to a cane, Eventually the knee became as good as new again, so much so that not only was he able to ride as he used to, but he even lived to break the same leg, just below the injured knee, and also recovered from that completely!

The fifties were crowded years for us. Our family was growing fast. For the next few years, after Beth's birth in 1948, either Jody or Betty gave us a new grandchild almost every year – Albert in 1950, Geddis in 1951, Bill in 1952, Jim in 1954, Danny in 1955, and Walter in 1956. Espy literally gloried in this bunch of babies. His grandchildren were the crowning joy of his life. I doubt if any man ever got more pleasure out of his grandchildren than Espy did. He lived to enjoy one more, Lucy's Annette, who was born in 1957, but he died just two months before the birth of her Elizabeth, and nine years before her Dave Espy, who was named for him.

Espy had loved his own children devotedly, but he had made them rather hard, at least, the two oldest. He had relaxed greatly with Lucy, and thoroughly enjoyed her babyhood, but grandchildren were still more enjoyable, more pleasure and less responsibility! He wanted his grandchildren with him constantly.

Beth had been our Baby since she was four months old. At that time Leon sent a very sick Betty and their baby girl home to us from California by plane. As the stewardess, holding the cunning fat baby in her pink "sleepers", followed Betty down the steps of the plane, Espy opened his arms to the little one, and she went to him unhesitatingly. From then on, she and the brothers and cousins who followed her, occupied first place in his heart and life.

The day following her return from California, we took Betty to the fine gynecologist and surgeon, Dr. Leighton Green, who had operated on me several times, for an examination. To our intense relief, he found that she did not need an operation. He prescribed complete bed rest and medication, so we took her home with us and put her to bed for several months. A treatment which did restore her to health, though she was never again the robust physical specimen she had been before Beth's birth.

We took care of "Buffy", as Mother immediately nicknamed the cute, fat baby, and thoroughly enjoyed the privilege of watching her growth and development. "Buffy" was a complete original, who always managed to be the center of interest where ever she was. From babyhood she began to exhibit personality traits, a strong will, a high temper, an intense craving for love and affection, a capacity for unexpected and often outrageous behavior, and a precocious mental development, traits which were to become increasingly noticeable as she grew older. Espy literally adored her, and lavished on her all the affection and attention that his rigid standards of parental duty had prevented his displaying to his own children.

She responded to his love, and enjoyed her primary place in his affections, though some years later she made one of her characteristic observations to her mother on the subject. Perhaps on this occasion she was bored by Espy's frequent insistence that she "give him some loving!", for Espy always enjoyed the physical demonstration of love, and, more and more as his grandchildren came along, he wanted to hold them in his arms, and have them shower him with hugs and kisses. At any rate, after one particularly demonstrative leave-taking, Buffy demanded of her mother, "Why does Espy take so much loving?" He was always Espy to her, as though she felt he was her especial property. After Albert's arrival, he and the rest of the grandchildren began to call him "Ga-Ga", later shortened to "Ga".

✦

Leon completed the semester at the University of California and returned to Texas to reenter the University of Texas, for he had found, to his surprise, that the professional education he got at Texas was superior to that of the far better advertised University of California. By this time Betty was well enough to return to Austin with him, and to take up her duties as wife and mother. They spent the next two years in Austin, where Leon completed work on two degrees, a B.A. in Geology and a B.S. in Petroleum Engineering.

We had not met Leon until Betty fell in love with him, but, as soon as they were married, our friendship with his parents began. Mr. Byerley was a successful independent oil operator, who had made and lost several fortunes in his adventurous lifetime, and Ruth, his wife, was a beautiful and admirable woman. Though Leon had been born in Arkansas, the family had moved to Midland when he was in the 5th grade. Mr. Byerley prospered in the oil development, which was just beginning, while Ruth became identified with all the programs of civic improvement in the growing town.

They quickly became warm friends of ours, and spent the 1949 Christmas holidays with us, when both sets of grandparents shared the pleasure of watching the adorable eleven-month-old baby enjoy her first Christmas. Ruth had bought Buffy an enormous doll, almost as big as she was, but the baby took no interest in it and preferred to swim in the sea of tissue paper with which the floor soon became littered. Buffy learned to walk that Christmas Day, tottering back and forth across the living room floor in excited delight between her Grandmother Ruth and me.

Mr. Byerley had cut all ties with his family when he ran away from home at 12, but Ruth had a large and close-knit family connection in California as I had in Texas. Three sisters and a brother and his wife often visited her, and after Betty and Leon's marriage, were usually brought to Ft. Davis for visits with us. We were closely associated with them until Ruth's untimely death in 1952.

Meanwhile my problems with my mother grew steadily worse, as those with Espy's mother gradually eased. Mrs. Miller reversed the usual procedure of aging and became a softer and better character as she grew older. This was largely due, I always felt, to the influence of her son-in-law, Tyrone Kelly, with whom she lived for the last twenty years of her life. So, though the tensions were lessened there, as Espy grew less subject to her dominating influence, they were increased at home, where Mother became more and more hurt and embittered, as she watched Espy and me drawn constantly closer together by our shared love and interests.

She went back to Marlin less and less as years went by. She bitterly resented being left alone during my necessary absences at the ranch, particularly in summer. Various members of her family, her brother, Harry Conoly, her sister-in-law, Nannie Foster, and her own sister Bess Bradford, were willing and eager to stay with her at these times, but, as her psychopathic jealousy of Espy gradually warped her mind, she became unable to even enjoy their company, and actually resented having them with her. She wanted only me, and she wanted me there constantly, tending to all her wants, taking her wherever she wanted to go, and waiting on her hand and foot. She resented sharing me with Espy, and the children.

I was finally forced to the realization that even her constant illnesses were brought on mainly by her determination to have all my attention centered on her. I am sure now that Mother had been a disturbed personality all her life, as many people of genius are, and she was a genius musically. From the time of my father's death at 14, she had become completely dependent on me, and had used her frequent illnesses and threats of death as a method of bending me to her will. I had inherited an independent mind and a strong will from my father, and I came to resent Mother's constant attempts to dominate my life while I was still just a girl.

Mother was the victim of a bad inferiority complex, though why is hard to understand, for she had a more than normal endowment of beauty, brains and talent. All of her life it was necessary for her to force others to obey her will, in order to justify to herself her course of conduct. She had done this with her family, and attempted to do it with my father, with a complete lack of success, for my father was too strong a character to allow even the wife he loved deeply to dominate him. This made their marriage a hectic one, and his premature death, at 39 was probably all that saved it from disaster.

Like many women of her generation, Mother had an abnormal attitude toward sex, and the physical demands of marriage were abhorrent to her. She had been willing for me to marry, but she was never reconciled to the actual fact of my marriage. She had not faced the possibility that I might come to love Espy as much as he loved me, and this was the thing that finally unhinged her precarious mental balance.

Even though she knew Espy to be a devoted husband and father, and though she realized she had been dependent on him for support for many years, she could feel nothing but blind hatred for him because he had, so she felt, stolen the love of her only child from her. I know now that Mother never loved me, nor anyone else, for she was incapable of unselfish love, and I know also that I had ceased to love her long before I met Espy Miller.

But my stern sense of filial duty and my pity for her desperate unhappiness made it impossible for me to do what Espy continually begged me to do – to send her back to Marlin. He even offered to finance her, if she would only leave us alone. But she refused to consider it, and I lacked the wisdom – perhaps the cruelty – to insist on it, though it would have meant a happier life for her as well as for us.

My greatest problem had always been to attempt to build a normal, happy home against and above this background of Mother's and Espy's mutual jealousy. It became no easier with the passing of years, though constant compromises enabled us to live with it. My relatives and friends understood the situation and many of them, over the years, tried to reason with Mother and to persuade her to a different course of behavior. The result was always the same – furious and lasting anger against the one who made the attempt – even her adored nephew, Conoly Bartlett!

The children understood the situation early, and, though they never failed to give Mother the attention and respect she demanded, their love and loyalty was always for their father. I was desperately afraid that the unnatural situation would warp their lives, but, fortunately, they were

Four Generations - Betty, Daughter with Beth,
and Munner (Mother Foster) - January 1953

able to live above it. Mother had always adored Clay, as she had adored many male relatives and friends except her husband and mine!

Clay was blessed with a large and tolerant nature, and, as he grew older, he was my greatest help in dealing with the warring personalities with whom we lived, and he was even able to love them both. Betty had gotten a mixed inheritance from both Mother and Espy and, from childhood, was passionately loyal to her father, even though they were so much alike in temperament that they frequently clashed. She resented Mother's attitude toward him and, though she never failed in respectful treatment of her, she lost all her affection for her. Nor had she any love for Espy's tyrannical old Mother.

In later years when Betty matured and our relationship changed from mother and daughter to that of understanding friends, she would say sadly, when I recalled how I had loved and had enjoyed my two grandmothers, "That is strange to me, for I never loved either of my grandmothers!"

Mother nearly lost her mind – a horrifying experience I still hate to recall – when she learned that I was pregnant with Lucy, and she had never forgiven the innocent child for being born. Luckily, Lucy shared Clay's tolerant temperament and she was from birth surrounded by the love of the rest of her family, so Mother's attitude never seemed to bother her.

As for me, I gradually became hardened to the situation. Though Mother never ceased to be the subject of bitter quarrels between Espy and me, our love for and need of each other grew constantly stronger in spite of this insoluble problem in our lives. I realized how much Espy loved me to put up with what he did for thirty years. Clay said to me once, "Mama, Daddy is a good man even to **live** in the same house with Munner", and he was right.

So I was thankful when the last of our children, Lucy, grew up and left for college, thus escaping the unwholesome atmosphere, as Betty and Clay had done when they married. I still had Espy to conciliate and keep in a good humor, for Espy was a jealous man, jealous of anything or anybody who took my attention from him, and he resented intensely Mother's increasing demands on me. It is amazing in retrospect to realize that in spite of this insoluble problem, we managed to lead active fairly normal and generally happy lives. In our social life we simply ignored the situation and were aided by understanding friends.

+

During Lucy's final year in High School – which she finished in three years instead of the usual four – the old home was made over. It had been in bad repair when Mother bought it twenty years before and had only been kept in livable condition by constant patching and repair. Major repairs were urgently needed.

Mother had long since exhausted my father's estate – except for a carefully guarded burial fund – and had no funds to make repairs, and Espy was unwilling to make the repairs while she still owned the house. She had steadfastly refused to relinquish ownership of it to me for fear that Espy would sell it and spend the money on the ranch! Finally, her Marlin relatives were able to persuade her to deed the house to me and, once this was done, Espy immediately began the job of making the house over. I sent Mother back to Marlin to stay while the work was going on.

A Houston contractor, Mike McCready (Kevin Bark's father), had recently moved to Ft. Davis to live. Espy engaged him to do over the house. The job was an extensive one, beginning with changing the ugly square roof to a high gable roof with three dormer windows in front. This almost doubled the size of the upstairs rooms. The whole house was replastered, inside and out, ceilings lowered in some rooms insulation and wiring installed, floor redone, a bath added upstairs and many closets built all over the house. Espy had a new well drilled in the back yard and a submersible pump installed.

C.E. Miller house in Fort Davis, pre 1950

To pay for this complete renovation of the house, Espy used the money he had received from a ten years oil lease on the ranch to Cities Service Oil Co., which amounted to $22,000. In later years, he was fond of saying to me, "you should not fuss about 27½% depletion allowance, Mama, because that's what built your house!" [52]

The work required four months to complete. For the first two months we attempted to live in the South bedroom, bath and kitchen, but when the dust from old plaster being knocked off the walls began to make Lucy sick, we rented a tiny apartment across the street from Mrs. Gibson and stayed there for two months more.

Two weeks before Christmas, 1952, we moved back home, though only the two south bedrooms downstairs, bath, back hall, kitchen and little dinning room had been completed, the rest of the house was a shambles. Jody, Clay and 18 months old Albert were coming in from the ranch to spend Christmas with us.

We put up a small Christmas tree in the corner of our bedroom, and were invited to Christmas dinner at the Kellys. Just four days before Christmas, Ruth Byerley died in Midland, of a hereditary heart trouble, after an agonizing illness. Betty and Leon rushed from Austin to Midland, left Buffy with Espy and me, and flew to California with Mr. Byerley for Ruth's funeral.

We brought Buffy home with us. She was not quite three, and that year all she wanted for Christmas was the "little baby Jesus"! She had gotten the idea from the tiny wax figure in an old crèche which had always decorated our tree. I was somewhat bothered about what her reaction would be when Santa failed to bring her "the little baby Jesus", but it turned out that she was quite satisfied with the baby doll he left for her.

It was a crowded Christmas, with seven of us jammed into two bedrooms, but that did not worry Beth and Albert. I shall never forget what glorious times those two babies had romping together. From then on, they have remained the best of friends.

Betty and Leon returned from California soon after Christmas, collected their baby and returned to Austin. In May, Leon completed

---

52 The Depletion Allowance in the oil industry is a tax deduction for the business to recover a percentage of their capital investment due to the permanent loss of the resource extracted.

work on his degrees, and they moved back to Midland to live with Mr. Byerley. Leon went to work for Honolulu Oil Co. as a geologist.

Work on the house was completed about the end of January. It was a joy to have a clean, comfortable and vastly more comfortable home. While work was in progress, we had Mother's old furniture done over at DuSang's in El Paso, so that it, like the house, was beautifully restored and good for another fifty years of service. [53] Mother came back from Marlin in February, and was never to leave Ft. Davis again until her death three years later.

Espy also built a new fence around the house. He was shocked when I insisted on a "corral fence", like those at the ranch, but after he was convinced of its suitability he did a careful and enduring job of building it. He sent to Kerrville for especially matched cedar stays, and selected each one for size before placing it in the line, while his Mexican helpers planted the stays deep in the ground and lashed them together securely with wire.

Whatever Espy built was built to last, and like all the other fences he built, this one was "hell for stout!" The fence created a lot of favorable comment and Espy was very proud of it, as he was of the home and of my flower garden. It always amused me, in later years, to

Miller Home, Fort Davis, Texas - June 1953

[53] Much of this furniture is still in use at the Miller home today.

Miller Ranch, Sierra Vieja Mountains - July 1952

observe the pride with which he showed our guests through "his garden"! [54]

It was well that we got the house built when we did, for the "Long Drought", which had begun in 1947, was increasing in severity every year, and had the oil lease money not been spent on the house when it was, it would inevitably have gone later to ease the ravages of drought on the ranch. This was the longest and most severe drought in recorded history.

For a 15-year period, with the exception of one or two normally wet years, rainfall was greatly deficient. In one two-year period, it was only 13 inches, considerably less than the normal annual rainfall. Like the Depression, one had to live through the Long Drought to know what it was like.

Espy often said that ranchmen could stand low prices, but it was drought that broke them. Only the hardiest, or the ones with the greatly envied "cross on oil" survived this one. The 1960 census showed the cattle population of Presidio County to be less than half of that of 1950, and this was typical of all ranch country in West Texas.

---

54 This fence built by Espy is still "Hell for stout."

Espy took every measure possible to meet the drought but by 1956, when the rainfall was 5 inches, his country was bare. The abundant feed crops produced by the irrigated farms saved the cattle on the Miller ranch, but there was not enough to support Espy's cattle also.

At first, he bought increasing amounts of feed, then he began to sell off more and more stock. Eventually in 1956, he sold everything off the ranch except 150 head of "seed-stock", his heifers and young cows, then he began a wide search for pasturage for them. He finally found grass at Ozona, where he leased a pasture from Alvin Harrell for this bunch of cows.

Alvin looked after the cattle for him, and we made frequent trips to Ozona to see about them. We kept the cattle in this leased pasture until the Long Drought was finally broken by good rains in the fall of 1958, then moved them back to the Vieja ranch. Again, a business deal, as in the case of the hunting lease to Elmer Ratcliff, resulted in a permanent friendship, as Alvin and Lucile Harrell became good friends.

+

Meanwhile, Lucy had spent a year and a half at North Texas (TSCW), and in February 1955, had transferred to the University of Texas. Espy and I went down to move her from Denton to Austin, and the three of us made a short trip down into the Rio Grande Valley between semesters. On our return to Austin, when we started to unload Lucy's trunk and other paraphernalia at her boarding house on White's Avenue, a good looking black headed boy from a boy's boarding house across the street came running over and carried her heavy things upstairs for us.

This was the start of another romance, for the boy was "Jake", Joseph William Jacobson, a Junior Engineering Student from San Antonio. By the end of the spring semester, they were engaged. Late that summer, I had an urgent invitation from Jake's mother in San Antonio to allow Lucy to accompany her and her daughter, Theda, and Jake on a three-week trip to California to visit relatives.

We gave our permission, thinking that this might break up the affair, but it did not turn out that way. After an enjoyable trip, on their way home, just prior to the opening of the fall semester at UT, they had an accident near Socorro, New Mexico; when the car turned over, Lucy's neck was broken.

We did not know this at first, however, as the doctors at the hospital in Socorro, where she spent the first two days after the accident, did not discover the break, even after numerous X-rays, and they assured us that her neck was only badly sprained. We left for Socorro immediately after receiving Jake's call about the accident and were allowed to bring Lucy home after forty-eight hours.

Two days later I carried her down to our Ft. Davis doctor, Don Gaddis, to get a medical excuse from him to enable her to register late at the University. He immediately recognized that the neck was broken and confirmed his diagnosis by X-rays. So we carried the child back to El Paso. In all we hauled her around over 800 miles, lying on the back seat of the car with a broken neck! Dr. David Cameron put her in a heavy body cast, which extended from the crown of her head to below her hips.

The break was between the 1st and 2nd vertebrae, and is the most dangerous, Don said, in the whole human body. Had the bone slipped and pinched the spinal cord, she would have been paralyzed; had it cut it, she would have died. Blessedly neither happened, and eventually she recovered completely, though she wore the body cast, or a heavier one the doctor put on six weeks later, for four months, and a stiff leather brace for five months more. It was nine long months before the neck finally healed.

With the heavy cast covering the entire trunk of her body, it was impossible for the child to wear her own clothes. All she could get over the cast during those dreadful months were her Daddy's size 16½ shirts and Betty's old maternity skirts. It was, of course, quite impossible for her to return to school, as she was almost helpless, could not bathe herself or comb her long hair.

At first, she had to have help to get into and out of bed, but Espy rigged up an iron bar at the head of her bed by which she soon learned to pull herself up. Her face was turned to the sky, so that she could not even read. But she was a brave girl. There was no complaint or self-pity, even when the pain and frustration were hard to endure. She wore the hideous cast gallantly, though it was unbelievably disfiguring.

I shall never forget sweet little Buffy's first reaction to it. She had always adored Lucy, as a little girl does a big one. While Lucy was in the cast that fall, Betty and Leo brought the children, for there were two boys now besides Buffy, Geddis, who was three, and a new baby named Dan, born just before Lucy's accident happened, up for a visit. Buffy came running into the kitchen where Lucy stood, gave one horrified, unbelieving gasp as she looked at her, then grabbed her tightly around the cast and hugged her as hard as she could!

Lucy was not able to do much because of the unnatural position of her head, so I read to her in my every spare moment, to try to help pass the long hours away. We got through a good number of the classics that fall. Jake came to see her at Thanksgiving and at Christmas, for the accident had not cooled the love affair.

I shall always believe that the sight of Lucy in that disfiguring cast hastened Mother's death, for she was a sight to shake the strongest nerves and Mother's nerves had never been strong. Not very long after Lucy's accident, Don Gaddis called me to his office to tell me that Mother was going to die soon.

I did not believe him, for I could not see a great change in her condition, although for the past year, she had grown weaker in mind and body. She became very quiet and passive, had little to say and ate almost nothing. I came to recognize the frequent "little" strokes that she was having. Lucy or I stayed with her constantly.

On the morning of Dec. 5, 1955, she died quietly in her sleep, a merciful release from the tragedy of her life. Espy, Clay and I went back to Marlin to bury her beside my father in the beautiful old Calvary Cemetery.

Jody brought her three boys to town, for Bill had arrived in 1952 and Jim in 1954, and they stayed with Lucy while we went to Marlin. Ever since the departure of my boarders in 1935, the big front room on the North of the house had been Mothers, and we had used the back room as a living room. As the family increased, the little family dining room became increasingly crowded.

While we were in Marlin, those two energetic girls, aided by some Mexican helpers, moved Mother's old furniture into the small bedroom across the hall, and converted her bedroom into the living room, and the former living room into the dining room. All of this was finished before I returned from Marlin, and it helped to ease the period of adjustment following Mother's death.

Though I grieved for the tragedy Mother's life had been, I was too honest not to realize that her death was not only release from a desperately unhappy life for her, but also for us. With her gone, the tension under which we lived for so many years was gone, and, for the remaining five years of Espy's life, we enjoyed the truly happy marriage that we could have had many years before except for poor mother.

Though she was endowed with talent, intelligence and charm far in excess of most people, she lacked an essential element for a successful life – she was completely unable to make herself or anyone else happy. I have prayed that she might be happy in Heaven, for she was never, I think, happy on this earth.

+

Events were crowding us fast now. Immediately after our return from Mother's funeral, we took Lucy to El Paso to have the cast removed. What a blessing it was to the child to have her young body free of that heavy cast! And what luxury to be able to take a bath in the tub and to have her long hair washed!

The break in the neck was still not healed, however, and Dr. Cameron insisted on her wearing a stiff leather collar for six months longer. He reluctantly allowed her to return to college in February 1956, and turned her over to the care of Dr. Sandi Esquivel in Austin. [55] It was May before the break finally healed, but she was a most fortunate girl to have passed thru this terrifying ordeal with no permanent injury.

The following spring Betty came down with hepatitis. I made several trips to Midland to look after her, but she was unable to get her strength back, so I finally brought her and the children home with me. We hired a good Mexican girl to take care of Dan and put Betty to bed.

Lucy and Jake were planning to be married the day after he received his Engineering degree in August. He already had a job with U.S. Steel in Pittsburgh. He was the first graduate of the U of T to be offered a job by U.S. Steel.

Lucy stayed in Austin for the first term of summer school, then came home and began preparations for her wedding. These were somewhat complicated by having a sick girl and a lively baby and two other children to look after, but somehow it all got done in time, and even Betty recovered enough to take her place as matron-of-honor.

It was, as Lucy often said afterwards, "Not a big society wedding, just a big *family* wedding!", and so it was, with a large group of our relatives in attendance, and about fifty of Jake's including one Jewish uncle, his wife and daughter from N.Y. City. Lucy and Jake left

55 Dr. Sandi Esquivel was a well-known orthopedic surgeon in Austin and former University of Texas athlete. (Obituary, Austin *American-Statesman*, April 8, 1969)

immediately for Pittsburgh, and Leon took his family home, and Espy and I were alone again – for the first time since the early months of our marriage. It was somewhat of a shock to be suddenly relieved of all the heavy responsibilities of my large family.

Espy often reminded me of the old joke about the wife who said mournfully to her husband, after the wedding of their last child, "Honey, you're all I've got left!" to which he replied, "I was all you had to begin with!"

The last five years of Espy's life were happy ones for us, and we were rarely separated. I was now free to go with him whenever and wherever he wanted me to – and I did. It seemed to me that we practically lived in the pickup, as we commuted back and forth between the ranch and town. But Espy was slowing down, much more than he liked to admit, and he was leaving more of the management and the hardest work to Clay.

In March of 1957 Espy and I made our first plane trip – to Pittsburgh to visit Lucy and Jake. They were lonely for the warm, friendly Southwest where they had both been reared, and we were lonely for them, so we flew up to see them, as Lucy positively put her foot down on her Daddy driving to Pennsylvania.

We took a plane in El Paso, and soon after we left Dallas, we encountered a tornado – though we did not know it at the time and thought the extreme roughness of the ride was normal. In Chicago, it was snowing heavily, and when we reached Pittsburgh, the plane could not land because of hazardous conditions. We flew on to Baltimore and landed, and several hours later, the whole group of passengers, (75 or 80) were put on a big bus, and sent back to Pittsburgh over the Pennsylvania turnpike, reaching our destination some twelve hours late.

The plane from Chicago had been full of commuters, executives, no doubt, all correctly dressed in dark suits and narrow brim hats. On the plane not a word of conversation had been exchanged with them, though I did notice some of them eyeing Espy. He did rather stick out in that crowd of pallid, conventional looking city men, with his impressive physique, ruddy color and soft Dobbs hat at the same rakish angle he always wore a hat!

During the long hours of the bus trip, the crowd got quite chummy, and all of them were soon calling Espy "Tex"! He was so unmistakably Western in appearance, yet completely individualized. With the exception of this somewhat shocking introduction to flying, the visit was a delightful one.

Jake and Lucy showed us all the sights, including a magnificent spring garden show at the Phipps Conservatory – a bit of Heaven under glass, with the wintriest scene I ever saw out-of-doors.

On the weekend they drove us to Washington – a never to be forgotten experience. I was awe stricken by the beauty and impressiveness of the Federal City in the first glory of spring. We spent much of our time in the National Gallery, for Espy loved art exhibits, and he never missed a museum if he could help it. We could have spent days at the Smithsonian, had we had the time. I shall always be grateful for that glimpse of our beautiful capitol.

+

With Clay and several good Mexicans living on the ranch, and with Keesey there much of the time, Espy was freer than he ever had been. This leisure time was largely devoted to Civic interests.

For years he had been active in the West Texas Historical and Scientific Society and had worked with the Fort Davis Historical Society since its beginning in 1953. This latter organization absorbed more and more of his interest and time in his last years. He did a lot of collecting for the museum – a job that came natural to him, as he had been a junk collector all his life! He made trips all over the country hunting up relics. His last project was setting up a pioneer kitchen in a room adjoining the main museum of the Society.

Espy had always had a sense of history, especially the local history of this country of which he had been a part for most of his life. He had an inexhaustible fund of stories about old times and old timers – many of which still had to be told privately out of respect for descendants! His Uncle Judge shared this interest in history.

Espy became a great reader as he grew older, especially of anything that dealt with the cattle industry or the history of the West. The first gift I made him, before we were married, was a copy of Capt. J.H. Cook's *Fifty Years on the Old Frontier*. This formed the basis of a nice little collection of books on the West, to which his family and friends frequently added.

He was still on the Board of Directors of the Highland Hereford Association, the Marfa Soil Conservation District, and the Federal Land Bank of Marfa. He made many trips in connection with these organizations. He went to the annual meetings of the Land Bank in Houston almost every year and was a close friend of officials of the Bank, Andrew Graves, Vic Johnson, Sterling Evans and others. His friendship with the astronomers at McDonald were many.

When the Harvard Radio Astronomy Observatory was established in Ft. Davis in 1956, Dr. Alan Maxwell, [56] the dynamic young director from New Zealand, was added to his list of friends, along with other members of its staff. His interest in the scientific work being done at both observatories was keen and he absorbed considerable knowledge from these contacts.

Most of the early cattlemen had no interest in anything beyond their own land and cattle. They looked on strangers and newcomers with distrust and dislike. As a rule they were selfish, self-centered and clannish. They saw every issue only as it affected their pocketbooks – much like the rest of mankind! They lived in this harsh desert land during the rough and dangerous years of settlement, and they had to be hard and tough even to survive! The fortunes some acquired were made by methods that often would not bear inspection. Most of them had "slung a long loop" and they were often laws unto themselves only.

The second generation of cattlemen in this country no longer had to fight off Indians and cattle thieves, but they still had to battle the constant enemies of the cowman – drought and depression. They were not as hard nor as lawless as the first generation had been and were more subject to the effects of civilization as it began to encroach on their isolated mountain fastness.

Some of them fought progress, in the form of railroads, good roads, better schools, etc., with all the resources at their command. Some tried desperately to keep all the land in their own hands. "All he wanted," Mr. John Z. Means was fond of saying, "was Jeff Davis County with a fence around it" While all Mr. Bill Jones wanted was just the land

56 Dr. Alan Maxwell was born in 1926 in Northcote, New Zealand. A musical prodigy, he gravitated to science, especially radio waves, a field of study derived from the development of radar during World War II. With a PhD from the University of Manchester he earned a position at Harvard University and was tasked with establishing the Harvard Radio Astronomy Station. He chose a valley location near Fort Davis that possessed minimal interference from manmade transmissions. Alan made numerous friends in the area and was a fixture at the Bloys Campmeeting until his death.

that joined his! But they were fighting a losing battle. The great days of the cattleman were over. Those who could not adjust to the rapidly changing conditions in the ranch business went down in defeat, and the great spreads began to be broken up by debt, division and death. The more enlightened cattlemen saw the handwriting on the wall, and were able to make the tremendous change from the days of the open range to modern scientific stock raising.

Espy was among the latter type. Because he was actually a survivor from an earlier era, by inheritance and by training, though not in age, his whole life was a struggle between the stubborn old ways of the cattle kings, that he had learned as a boy, and the continual expansion and enlightenment of his mind by ever widening ideas, interests and associations. His work with civic agencies brought him constantly in contact with brilliant specialists in many fields, and he learned from all of them.

He learned reluctantly, it is true, for it was hard for him to relinquish the ingrained prejudices of another age. His family also broadened him. He violently resisted many of my liberal ideas in the early years of our marriage – ideas that he gradually, almost unconsciously, came to accept later on. This was a mutual process, for I had my full share of prejudices too – usually exactly opposite to Espy's! – but many of them were softened or changed after years of association with him.

I have always felt that the most civilizing influence in Espy's life was his love for his children and grandchildren. Because he loved them so devotedly and because he was so eager for them to become the best people possible, he shared their ever enlarging interests and became a more enlightened and unselfish parent. In later life, Espy was grounded by the love of his large and growing family and by the affection of a host of friends. He literally bloomed in this benign atmosphere and became steadily more outgoing and warm hearted and more thoughtful of others.

Nothing showed this more than his attitude toward his grandchildren. They were the greatest joy of his life. He wanted them around him constantly. As a result, they felt that "Ga" existed primarily for their entertainment. He was still trying to "train them up in the way they should go", especially in teaching them to ride a horse, almost up until

Espy with his grandchildren Albert, Bill, Geddis, and Beth -
January 1953

he died. He was constantly on a search for suitable horses for them, even though faithful old "Tajonie" was still in use for the youngest ones.

It was a sight to see Espy on placid old Streak, with the youngest child in the saddle in front of him, the next youngest sitting behind the saddle and clinging with small arm to Ga's wide girth, and the third youngest on old Tajonie in his rear, lead by a string which Espy was holding, and the rest of the crew following behind.

Espy was in his element then, as he encouraged their efforts and yelled instruction to them alternately. I was always fearful that he would have an accident trying to cope with so many little ones on horseback, but he never did, though he did let one or two roll out of a pickup! Under his competent instruction, all his own children and

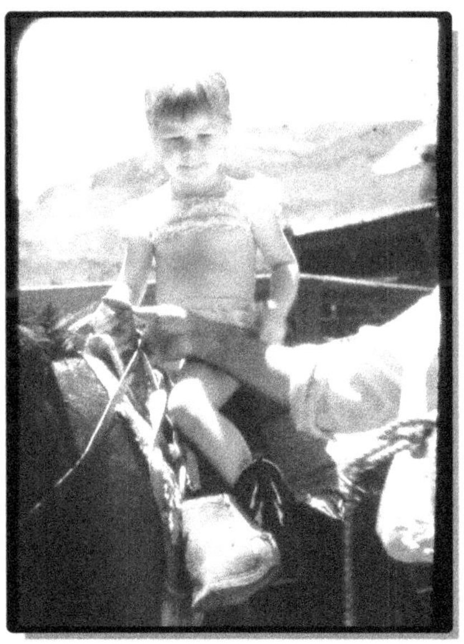

Beth on "Tajorz" - June 1953

Beth and Geddis - June 1955

Espy and Clay with Albert, Bill, and Jim - June 1955

the first eight grandchildren, his nephews and many others learned to be competent riders.

Though he was indulgent to them, he expected them to mind and obey orders. He did not hesitate to punish them when he thought they needed punishment. I recall an incident that happened one summer while

Clay, Espy, and Betty on horseback

the Byerleys were visiting the ranch along with the Clay Millers. Like any bunch of children, the young fry frequently got into mischief.

Great was Espy's indignation when he went out one afternoon and discovered the whole bunch "chunking" rocks thru the windows of his shop. Beginning with Beth, the oldest, he grabbed and thoroughly spanked each child in turn – and they did not repeat that bit of vandalism again!

He could entertain them endlessly with tales of his early life and experiences, especially by exciting yarns about hunting expeditions which were altogether products of his imagination. The little ones loved these thrilling recitals. I shall never forget the last trip Espy made into town from the ranch, following a severe heart attack the night before. We had Jim and Walty, then five and three, with us at the ranch. While I drove the pickup, Espy sat with a boy on each knee, telling them tales of bear hunts all the way into Valentine, though he was suffering intense pain in his chest.

This growing benevolence in Espy's character was also noticeable outside his family. He was born an extrovert, and he had always liked all kinds of people, but in his last years, he had more time to enjoy them. Clay had gradually assumed most of his duties on the ranch, especially those of a physical nature, for we all realized that, in spite of his robust appearance, Espy's health was rapidly failing.

It was a constant effort to keep his diabetes under control, a constant struggle against gaining more weight, and there was an increasing exhaustion after any exertion. His physical strength and endurance had always been a matter of pride with him, and it was humiliating to him to realize that he could no longer do the strenuous things he had always done. Increasingly, Clay did the hard work and Espy was largely relegated to the role of boss! He had always been one of the world's best bosses!

For the last twenty years of his life, he was constantly under the care of doctors, as they strove to control his diabetes, but the insidious disease was slowly taking its toll on his energy and strength. Since he was able to do less at the ranch, we spent more and more time in Ft. Davis, where his interests in people and in civic improvement gradually made him a sort of unofficial, one man, "Chamber of Commerce". In a real sense, he became "Mr. Fort Davis". How many people remarked to me after his death, "Fort Davis will never be the same again without Espy!"

For years Espy had been worried, as were all land owners in the West, over the problem of the heavy Federal inheritance taxes on land. Fred LaLanne of the Marfa Federal Land Bank, Frank Barton, President of the Marfa National Bank and others had long advised him that his wisest course would be to sell the ranch to Clay before he died, in order to lessen the inheritance taxes.

So in 1957, we did sell the Vieja ranch to Clay. Espy, Clay and their advisor worked out an arrangement by which Espy leased the ranch back from Clay, then employed him as manager – an arrangement that equalized the payments, lease and wages. This worked so successfully that I have continued the same arrangement since Espy's death.

Several years prior to this, Espy and Keesey had sold the nine sections comprising the farms to their respective sons, Clay and K.K. Espy and Keesey remained partners on the rest of the Miller ranch. All these involved partnerships worked harmoniously, and were operated as a unit in actual practice, although the finances were separate.

At the time of the sale of the ranch, Espy and I gave Clay the full extent of the gift allowed by the Federal Inheritance Tax laws. In his will, Espy forgave Clay half of his debt remaining on the Vieja ranch, as I also will do with my half on my death. Espy willed his one fourth interest in the Miller ranch to his daughters, as I also have done in my will. We wrote identical wills to this end. We had seen too many families falling out over inherited property, so we obtained the full and free consent of all three children to this disposition of ours. Above all things we wanted that they should never lessen their love for each other by a quarrel over what small inheritance we were able to leave them.

✦

Espy had one more accident in the last years of his life. In attempting to help me hang out quilts to sun on a spring day, he slipped on a wet spot on the sidewalk and broke his leg. It was the same leg on which he had had the knee operation several years before. Again, it had to be put in a cast, and again he was on crutches for several months, and again he made a compete recovery.

Also, in those last years we made a most enjoyable trip to California with Betty and Leon. While Leon attended the sessions of a

Petroleum Engineers Meeting, we had a delightful visit with Lucy and Jake and little Annette in their home in Bellflower.

This trip stands out in my memory as one of the most pleasant ones I ever made because Leon was such a careful, considerate driver. I really enjoyed the trip, something I was never able to do when Espy was at the wheel. His driving grew steadily worse with age, as his reflexes slowed and his sense of speed lessened. We made many visits to Midland in those last years, and we rarely left the Byerley home without Betty in tears, pleading with her Daddy to drive more slowly and carefully. This had no effect whatsoever except to irritate Espy. He would rarely let me drive, for he always claimed that my driving made him nervous.

But in his final year, we made numerous trips to El Paso for treatment by a specialist of pyorrhea [57] a condition which Don Gaddis had discovered that Espy had. This specialist, Dr. Peckett, was a sadist who actually seemed to enjoy making the treatments as painful as possible. Espy would not let me drive up to El Paso for these treatments, but, when they were over, he would fall into the side seat, in agony as the opiate wore off, and allow me to drive home without protest. These treatments, incidentally, were completely unsuccessful, as Don Gaddis discovered in Espy's last days. This was one of the few unpleasant experiences we ever had with a doctor and it was not peculiar to us, as other of Dr. Peckett patients had the same experience.

Although I was well aware of the general deterioration of Espy's health, it was not until the fall of 1959, that I first suspected heart trouble. He began to complain frequently of indigestion, and to have sharp pains in his chest after any unusual exertion. I tried to save him in every way I could, especially in the heavy lifting. Our trips back and forth to the ranch involved much carrying in and out of suitcases, cartons of food, clothes and supplies. As soon as I realized that any lifting caused Espy chest pains, I tried to keep him from doing any of it, but it was hard to do, for it hurt his male pride to have his wife doing these jobs for him.

In spite of his condition, which he constantly tried to minimize, Espy was determined to attend the annual meeting of the directors of the Federal Land Bank in Houston late in January 1960. We drove to San Antonio, where I stopped for a visit with my cousins, Beth and Connaly

---

57 "Pyorrhea" is also known as periodontitis, a severe gum disease.

Carmichael, while Espy flew on to Houston for the meeting. On his return, he drove home and a few days later we attended the annual banquet of the Highland Hereford Association in Alpine.

By this time I had become so worried about Espy's constant chest pains that I insisted on his going to see Don Gaddis. Don at once increased his insulin dosage and put him on a starvation diet. But it was too late. The chest pains continued and finally, the first week in March, he had his first definite heart attack.

It happened one night at the ranch, when Jim and Walty were with us. The following morning, I drove them all to town and left the boys in Valentine with Jody. Don came to the house to see Espy as soon as we reached Ft. Davis and put him to bed. After a more severe attack the next day, he moved him down to the little hospital he was then operating in Fort Davis. Though the electrocardiogram registered only a "mild" attack, Don realized his danger, and ordered complete rest and quiet.

Although we had excellent nurses with him, either Clay or I sat by his bedside constantly – relieved for brief rest periods by Audrey or Lillian. Espy did not want me to leave him, and I did so as briefly as possible. On my return to the sick room, his dear face would break into a smile and the light of love would beam from his eyes. Never in our life together was I so aware of the deep love between us as in those hours.

The Byerleys came up to see him, and because of Espy's pleading, Don reluctantly allowed all seven little grandchildren to file into his room and to talk to him for a few minutes. It was a solemn ritual for the little ones, but a great joy to their dying grandfather.

After a week in the hospital, clots began to form – a bad one in the right leg. Don urged us to allow him to call in consultation, to which we quickly assented. He called an internalist from El Paso, Dr. Sterling Martin, who came the following day. The doctors agreed that an operation to implant a plastic artery in his leg and thus by-pass the clot, was the only possibility of saving his life.

During the night, Espy was near death several times, but since he was still alive at dawn, the doctors insisted on starting for El Paso where the operation would be performed. I was much opposed for I knew he was dying and I felt that the trip would only subject him to useless suffering. But you do all you can to prolong the life of a loved one.

An ambulance carried Espy and the two doctors to El Paso, with Keesey and Lillian and me following in their car. At Van Horn, another clot struck Espy, completely paralyzing his left side and rendering him unable to speak. We rushed on to Providence Hospital in El Paso, where teams of doctors and nurses worked incessantly with Espy in an effort to save his life – employing every technique known to medical science. I stood by his bed, and held the poor restless right hand, which never ceased its wild movement until he died.

While doctors and nurses fought for his life, friends and relatives came and went, offering sympathy, but it was obvious that the end was near. I bitterly resent all the expedients that doctors and nurses were using on his poor body in an effort to prolong his life, for in spite of Dr. Martin's assurances that he might recover, I knew that he would not and I wanted him to die in peace. Death came at five o'clock on March 12th when his heart gave out.

I had been by his side almost continually for forty eight hours, without sleep and with little rest, and, though I was numb with exhaustion and grief, I was completely composed and in no need of the tranquilizer Dr. Martin insisted on giving me. Keesey and Lillian took me from the hospital to the home of my cousins, Willet and Evelyn Foster, where I called the children, and later on that night, they drove me back to Ft. Davis.

We reached home about three and found a crowd of relatives and friends waiting. Lucy and Jake were unable to come, since she was expecting her second baby in a few weeks, but the rest of our family and many relatives and friends came to his funeral two days later. The service was held at the Baptist church, where he had been a member most of his life.

How does one judge a successful life? Though Espy's life was confined to an isolated, thinly populated section of the country, and did not touch great numbers of people, and, though he never became rich or famous, I, who knew him most intimately, would call his a successful life and a significant one. He worked hard for those values he believed in, and he left a record of unselfish service to his family and community that anyone might envy. He made and kept a host of friends during his life, although there were people he did not like or approve of, for Espy had plenty of prejudices, as far as I know, he never had an enemy. He was honest and honorable in business dealing, and warm and friendly in personal relations.

By hard work, severe economy and good business judgement and without any outside help, he acquired and kept a ranch at a period when that was an almost unheard-of accomplishment. Unlike most people, he became more open minded and tolerant as he grew older, and he never ceased to be interested learning new things and in meeting new people.

But it was within his own family that his success was the greatest. Although he may not have always been a wise parent (and who is?), he was always a loyal and devoted father and grandfather, and his entire married life was devoted to doing what he felt was best for his family. He set them a splendid example of love and devotion, and he reaped a rich reward in their undying love.

Although our marriage was always a stormy one, as it inevitably would have been between two people as temperamentally different and as strong willed as Espy and I were, it was never a dull one. I would not change it for any other marriage I ever knew. I only wish that I had been as wise when I was young as I am now. How much unhappiness I might have saved us both! But, in spite of all our troubles, we had our full share of happiness.

Few women have been blessed with the all-absorbing devotion that Espy gave me, and few women ever had such a wonderful, outrageous, exciting and loving man for a husband as I did. Espy was the most vital person I ever knew. He pulled me out of my indifference and self-centeredness into life and love, and taught me to share his passionate interest in people and in life itself.

Losing such a companion, after almost thirty-five years of married life, was as acute a physical loss as losing an arm or an eye would have been. Part of us dies, I think, when a loved one dies, and I have never felt fully alive since he left me.

Nevertheless I would not have had him live any longer than he did – paralyzed and impotent as he was in those last hours. He was too vital a person to have endured invalidism. I shall always be grateful to God that he was able to live a fairly normal and active life until within ten days of his death.

The life force was stronger in Espy than in anyone else I ever knew. Everybody who knew him felt it, and responded to its stimulation, and it was his best gift to the family he loved so well.

+

Espy with Albert, April 1952

Daughter in her garden

*The Davis Mountains view from the
Miller Ranch, November 1965*

Cattle on the Miller Ranch, November 1966

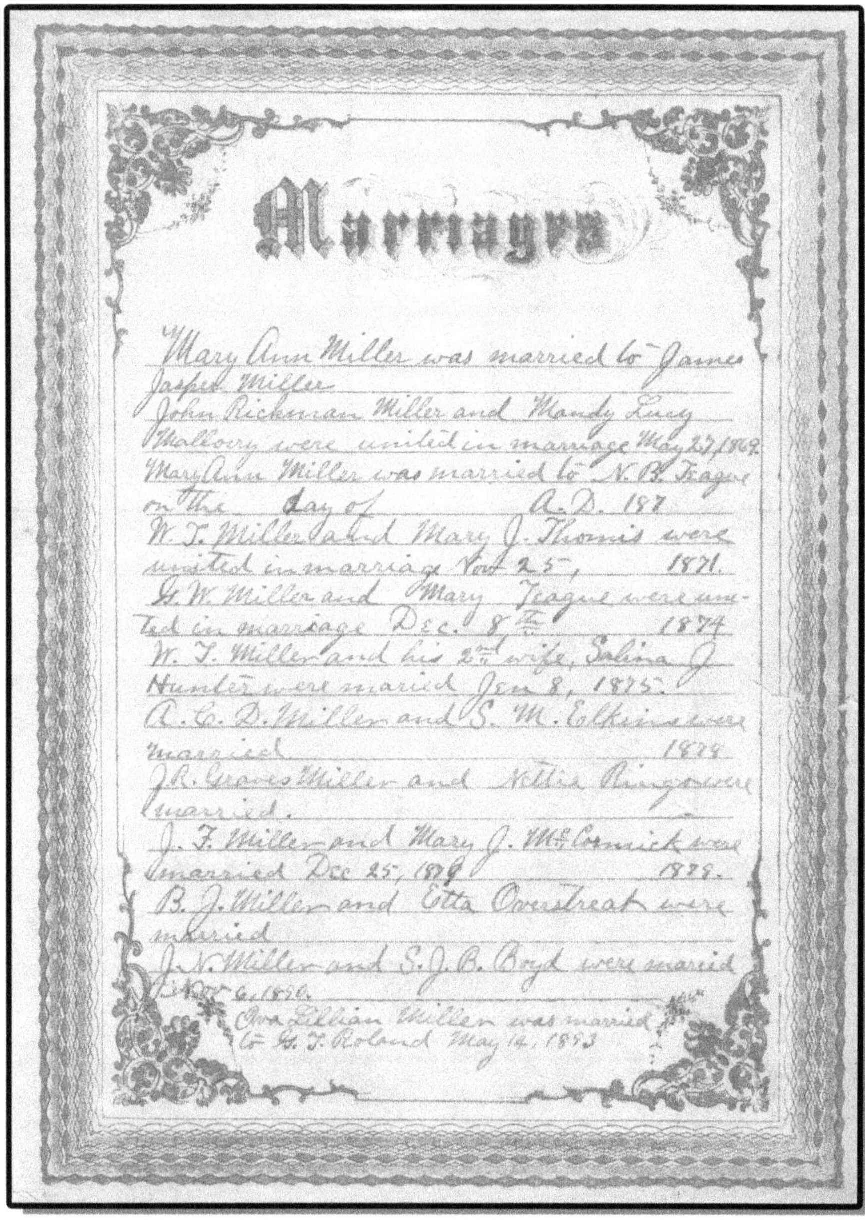

Miller Marriages 1869 to 1893, from John Kimsey Miller Family Bible, image courtesy of Michele Miller Browning

Appendix 1

The Families

Clay Espy Miller (Espy)

While the Miller's and the Espy's are among the largest families in Jeff Davis County, the following is the genealogy of the generations included in Lucy's memoir.

1. Henry Clay Espy 1849 - 1893

m. Rowena Amelia [Marley] Espy 1848 - 1936

    2. James Able Espy 1873 - 1937

    2. Lena Elizabeth [Espy] Miller 1874 - 1962

    m. Walter Spurgeon Miller 1871 - 1936

        3. Rosalie Miller 1892 - 1893

        3. Clay Espy Miller 1895 - 1960

        m. Lucy Conoly [Foster] Miller 1902 - 1994

            4. Clay Espy Miller, Jr. b. 1926 - 2017

            m. 1949 Jo Ellen "Jody" [Canada] Miller 1925 - 2018

                5. Albert Walter Miller 1950

                5. William Russell Miller 1952

                5. James Clay Miller 1954

                5. Walter Leon Miller 1956

            4. Mary "Betty" Elizabeth [Miller] Byerley 1927 - 1996

            m. 1948 Leon Geddis Byerley, Jr. 1925 - 2020

                5. Ruth Elizabeth [Byerley] Francell 1948

                5. Leon Geddis Beyerley III 1952

                5. Daniel Clay Byerley 1956

             4. Lucy Mildred [Miller] Jacobson 1935 - 2017

            m. 1956 Joseph William "Jake" Jacobson 1933 - 1985

                5. Lucy Annette Jacobson 1957 - 1980

                5. Ionia Elizabeth Jacobson 1960

                5. Dave Espy Jacobson 1969

Henry Clay Espy and Rowena Amelia Marley Espy had six children. Besides Lena, who married Walter Miller, there was Jim, Joe, Kate, Mary Sargent ("Sargie"), and Robert Henry. Robert Henry was known as "Judge" and he and his wife Beulah were close friends with Espy and Lucy. Joe, who Lucy felt often took advantage of her husband is often mentioned by Lucy as "Espy's Uncle Joe."

Walter Spurgeon Miller and Lena Elizabeth Espy had two other children following Espy. John Keesey Miller (1902-1981) and Audrey Elizabeth Miller (1915-2004). Keesey, as he was known, graduated from Texas A&M in 1924 with a degree in Mechanical Engineering and purchased the Fort Davis Auto Company and Garage. He also operated a heavy equipment company until World War II. In 1937 he and Espy purchased the adjacent Otis Kimball Ranch. He married Lillian Yarbro in 1929, and they had one son John Kimball.

Audrey Miller married Tyrone Kelly who owned and operated the Union Mercantile. They had three sons, Robert, John, and Thomas.

Lucy Conoly Foster (Daughter)

Lucy's family was centered in, and was a large part of, Marlin, Texas. The Foster's and the Conoly's, including the Bartlett's were an important part of Marlin life, and provided Lucy with any number of cousins, aunts, and uncles. Her father, Albert, was a Foster and her mother was a Conoly. The best way to understand how Lucy grew up and these family relationships is to read *The Marlin Compound: Letters of a Singular Family* by Frank Calvert.

Miller Family, image courtesy of Michele Miller Browning

*John Keesey, Audrey Elizabeth, Walter S.,
Clay Espy, Lena Elizabeth Miller*

The descendants of Walter Spurgeon Miller and Lena Elizabeth Espy Miller. Circa 1958 (not shown John "Kimball" Miller only child of Keesey and Lillian Miller)

Appendix 2

Dispatch

Lucy Foster Miller: A lady ahead of her times

EDITOR'S NOTE: This is the third in a series of articles by the staff at Fort Davis National Historic Site in recognition of Women's History Month. It pays tribute to an outstanding West Texas woman.

She planned to spend only a few days in Fort Davis. It was the summer of 1923, and Lucy Foster, a recent graduate of the University of Texas and the proud owner of a new Model T Ford was on her way to El Paso with her mother and two friends to meet her fiance.

What a sensation the group caused as they drove into town. They were the first group of women to make the trip from Austin to Fort Davis by automobile and it had taken them five days. During their stay in Fort Davis, Lucy met Espy Miller, a young rancher, and son of the proprietors of the Limpia Hotel . Two years later, she gave up her position as Extension Specialist in History and Economics in the loan department of the University of Texas Library to marry the young Mr. Miller and to make her home in the wilds of West Texas.

Lucy Foster Miller was born in Marlin, Texas on January 26, 1902, the first and only child of Dr. Albert Foster and Lucy Conoly Foster. She spent most of her childhood in the small town of Caldwell where she says she was more of a tomboy than a proper young lady.

Her father's death in 1916, however, brought her carefree childhood to an end, for Lucy's mother now became dependent on her for support and guidance.

Soon after Lucy and Espy married, Espy purchased part of the Finley Ranch, southwest of Valentine, and moved his bride and his mother-in-law to one of the small officers' quarters that was part of old Camp Holland. for Lucy and her mother it seemed like "the end of the world."

From January until June neither woman left the ranch. It was a very difficult time for all. Mother Foster, accustomed to city life in Austin, regarded herself as an alien. It was up to Lucy to entertain her and at the same time make a happy home for her husband.

In October, 1926, Lucy, who is affectionately called "Daughter" by members of her family, Espy, new baby Clay, and Mother Foster moved to the old Vieja ranch house located a little closer to town.

These quarters were more comfortable, but they, too, were isolated, and with the addition of a daughter, Betty, the work seemed endless. Reading and planting flowers became Lucy's only sources of entertainment.

A major earthquake in August, 1931 severely damaged the Miller's home. The family narrowly escaped injury fleeing the house just seconds before the chimneys came crashing down. While doing repairs on the house, Espy moved his family first to the hotel in Fort Davis and then into two tents he borrowed and set up at the ranch. After repairs were finished, Lucy reluctantly moved back inside.

When Clay was seven, the family moved to Fort Davis for him to begin school. Soon the enterprising Lucy opened a boarding house. As many of the boarders were school teachers, their departure during the summer afforded Lucy, grandmother, and children the opportunity to join Espy at the ranch.

With the arrival of a third child, Lucy decided to retire from the boarding house business, and devote her energies to community organizations. Already active in the Presbyterian Church, she joined the Fort Davis Study Club and the P.T.A. She was the moving power behind Barry Scobee's project of planting trees on the Courthouse lawn, and she was responsible for establishing the first study club library. She and Espy were founding members of the Fort Davis Historical Society.

At the age of 89, Lucy Foster Miller is a vibrant and stimulating woman. She is never without a book in hand and can put many a younger person to shame when it comes to discussing current events or politics. She was one of the first "women libbers" in West Texas, and has had more of an influence on this rugged land, than the land has had on her. Lucy Miller is truly a lady ahead of her times.

Transcription: Newspaper article from Davis Mountain Dispatch, 1991

Lucy Foster Miller: A lady ahead of her times

EDITOR'S NOTE: This is the third in a series of articles by the staff at Fort Davis National Historic Site in recognition of Women's History Month. It pays tribute to an outstanding West Texas woman.

She planned to spend only a few days in Fort Davis. It was the summer of 1923, and Lucy Foster, a recent graduate of the University of Texas and the proud owner of a new Model T Ford was on her way to El Paso with her mother and two friends to meet her fiancé.

What a sensation the group caused as they drove into town. They were the first group of women to make the trip from Austin to Fort Davis by automobile and it had taken them five days. During their stay in Fort Davis, Lucy met Espy Miller, a young rancher, and son of the proprietors of the Limpia Hotel.

Two years later, she gave up her position as Extension Specialist in History and

Economics in the loan department of the University of Texas Library to marry the young Mr. Miller and to make her home in the wilds of West Texas.

Lucy Foster Miller was born in Marlin, Texas on January 26, 1902, the first and only child of Dr. Albert Foster and Lucy Conoly Foster. She spent most of her childhood in the small town of Caldwell where she says she was more a tomboy than a proper young lady.

Her father's death in 1916, however, brought her carefree childhood to an end, for Lucy's mother now became dependent on her for support and guidance.

Soon after Lucy and Espy married, Espy purchased part of the Finley Ranch, southwest of Valentine, and moved his bride and his mother-in-law to one of the small officer's quarters that was part of old Camp Holland. for Lucy and her mother it seemed like "the end of the world."

From January until June neither woman left the ranch. It was a very difficult time for all. Mother Foster, accustomed to city life in Austin, regarded herself as an alien. It was up to Lucy to entertain her and at the same time make a happy home for her husband.

In October, 1926, Lucy, who is affectionately called "Daughter" by members of her family, Espy, new baby Clay, and her Mother Foster moved into the old Vieja ranch house located a little closer to town.

These quarters were more comfortable, but they, too, were isolated, and with the addition of a daughter, Betty, the work seemed endless. Reading and planting flowers became Lucy's only sources of entertainment.

A major earthquake in August, 1931 severely damaged the Miller's home. The family narrowly escaped injury fleeing the house just seconds before the chimneys came crashing down. While doing repairs on the house, Espy moved his family first to the hotel in Fort Davis and then into two tents he borrowed and set up at the ranch. After repairs were finished, Lucy reluctantly moved back inside.

When Clay was seven, the family moved to Fort Davis for him to begin school. Soon the enterprising Lucy opened a boarding house. As many of the boarders were school teachers, their departure during the summer afforded Lucy, grandmother, and children the opportunity to join Espy at the ranch.

With the arrival of a third child, Lucy decided to retire from the boarding house business, and devote her energies to community organizations. Already active in the Presbyterian Church, she joined the

Fort Davis Study Club and the P.T.A. She was the moving power behind Barry Scobee's project of planting trees on the Courthouse lawn, and she was responsible for establishing the first study club library. She and Espy were founding members of the Fort Davis Historical Society.

At the age of 89, Lucy Foster Miller is a vibrant and stimulating woman. She is never without a book in hand and can put many a younger person to shame when it comes to discussing current events or politics. She was one of the first "women libbers" in West Texas, and has had more of an influence on this rugged land, than the land has had on her. Lucy Miller is truly a lady ahead of her times.

Appendix 3

CLAY ESPY MILLER

The historical societies and the civic organizations of the Davis Mountains-Big Bend area lost one of their most enthusiastic and devoted supporters when Espy Miller died on March 12, 1960. With all his busy ranch work, he always found time to participate actively in the West Texas Historical and Scientific meetings at Sul Ross State College, the Fort Davis Historical Society, and the Mile High Club of Fort Davis.

He was an industrious gatherer of exhibits for the museums of these societies. The late Victor J. Smith, the one-man builder of the Big Bend Memorial Museum on the Sul Ross State College campus, stated many times that Espy Miller was his most faithful and generous contributor to the museum. Once Mr. Miller made a trip to Barstow, solely to pick up an ancient high-wheeled bicycle for the college museum. This bicycle had been brought to West Texas by an early settler, and in 1900, it had been ridden over roads of deep sand from Barstow in Reeves County to Monahans in Ward County. He made trips to the Balmorhea area and collected historical relics for the Fort Davis Museum.

After his death, the Fort Davis Society dedicated a room in its museum to Mr. Miller. This room is a replica of a pioneer living room and kitchen with a cracked cookstove, a bedstead, table, dishes, chairs, coffee grinder and other such antiques, most of which Espy had collected.

Espy Miller came to Fort Davis in a wagon with his parents, Mr. and Mrs. Walter S. Miller when he was only five months old. He was born October 23, 1895, in San Saba, Texas, and the date of his arrival in the little still-pioneer mountain town was on April 1, the next year. Half a century later he joked about the April Fools trick he played on the Fort Davis people.

In Espy's youth the frontier days were fading, the old Fort was empty of soldiers, branding someone else's cattle was on the wane, and the door of time had opened and let in a new century and new ways. But the boy, as he grew up, learned of the landmarks of the earlier years, learned to love them, and set out to preserve their history.

For one thing, as a boy he watered range cattle with a rope and bucket, day after day, at Van Horn wells near Lobo, where countless cavalry and teams of westward-bound wagons on the Great Military Road from San Antonio to El Paso had stopped a thousand times for water. Even then Espy sensed the romance and adventure of this area.

Those same soldiers and wagons had traveled through the Indian haunted gorge of Limpia canyon's Wild Rose Pass, and before Espy was of voting age he himself had hauled wood through the narrow and hazardous passage for his uncle, Joe W. Espy, one time with the wagon afloat on rolling flood waters and the mules half swimming. Espy would speak of the incident with backward-looking memories in his eyes.

Mr. Miller and Miss Lucy Conoly Foster were married July 18, 1925. Shortly after that he bought the old Holland ranch west of Valentine, in the shade of the Rimrock. There, seven years before, the War Department had built a stone fort as a protection against the Mexican troubles of that time, and had abandoned it soon afterward. Mr. and Mrs. Miller spent the first months of their marriage in one of the officers' quarters there. Perhaps living on this historic site intensified his interest in the frontier history of this area.

As a cattleman, Clay Espy Miller joined the Highland Hereford Breeders Association and was twice its president and a long-time director. In 1949 he was awarded the first plaque that the organization issued for his energetic work in soil conservation. While he was interested in preserving the history of the past, he was progressive and modern in his ranching and cultural projects. He was chairman of the board of supervisors of the Highland Soil Conservation District for three five-year terms. For twenty years he was director in the Marfa Federal Land Bank and often was its spokesman at statewide conferences.

Espy and his brother, J. Keesey Miller, bought land adjacent to the Holland Ranch and together they developed a considerable feed grain irrigation project, almost in sight of Van Horn Wells. It is still in profitable production.

Unquestionably, one of Mr. Miller's most admirable characteristics was his liking for his fellowman. He possessed the enviable knack of getting acquainted with strangers. Friends said of him, "He's a top hand to travel around with, because you see more, hear more, and meet more people than you ever could alone." His friendly manner and ready smile attracted people. Too, he was a facile raconteur and always had a story on tap about some early history of the Davis Mountains area. Mr. Scobee states that Espy Miller was never too busy with his ranch work to hesitate about joining him on a trip to some West

Texas site to gather historical material. Fortunately, his closest running mate for several years before his death was Barry Scobee, and Mr. Scobee has preserved much of the history which Espy Miller gathered during his lifetime.

Written as part of a group of biographical sketches by Bryan Wildenthal, Published in the Sul Ross State College Bulletin of the West Texas Historical and Scientific Society in Alpine, Texas Number 19 Vol. XLIII No.3, page 30, 31, and 32 on September 1, 1963

Beth Francell, the oldest grandchild of Lucy and Espy Miller, was raised in Midland but spent time in Fort Davis with her Lucy, especially after Espy died. She graduated with honors from the University of Texas, was a founding member of the Wichita County Heritage Society using her talents to create state historic markers for Wichita Falls. She was the founding Director of the Ferrill-Wilson Museum, a living history farm, in Plano, Texas. She attended the School of Landscape Architecture at the University of Texas at Arlington and in 1996 she and her husband purchased her grandparent's historic home in Fort Davis. For twenty-five years, following Lucy's love of gardening, she owned REBloom Designs. Currently, when not researching family history and gardening, she pursues her other passion, painting in pastel.

www.ingramcontent.com/pod-product-compliance
Lightning Source LLC
Chambersburg PA
CBHW051509050726
47594CB00010B/4027